"Why Didn't Anyone Tell Me helps bι
sensitivity, honesty, and a 'tell it like it is' approach.
**-Shoshana S. Bennett, Ph.D., President of Postpartum Assistance
for Mothers and co-author of *Beyond the Blues***

"The stories Bowden tells, in addition to her reflections on the circumstances that each mother faced, contain not only realistic depictions of motherhood, but also helpful insights and strategies to cope with being a new mom. This book has real news for new moms."
-Claudia Heilbrunn, Life Coach for first-time moms

"These courageous women do not grab the headlines, but grab our hearts and our attention. They speak for the vast majority of new mothers everywhere who have discovered that this highly charged, emotional phase of life is one for which most are unprepared. Bowden drives home the old adage that education is the first line of defense."
**-Ilyene Barsky, MSW,
Founder and Director of The Center for Postpartum Adjustment**

"As a birth and postpartum doula, I feel this book is a 'must have' in a new parent's library. The days and weeks following the birth of a baby are not always as easy as some make it seem. In this wonderfully written book, women can find first-hand information, advice, and resources about the possible struggles they may face."
**-Jennifer Rode,
Certified Doula (Doulas of North America)**

Bowden's book captures my own personal reaction to becoming a mother nearly thirty-five years ago. The theme throughout the book is the importance of mothering our mothers. I am confident that the voices crying out for help in Bowden's book will help ease the adjustment for families yet to be born.
**-Jane I. Honikman,
Founder of Postpartum Support International**

Printed in the United States of America.

Booklocker.com, Inc.
2006

WHY DIDN'T ANYONE TELL ME?

True Stories of New Motherhood

by

Melanie Bowden

Dedicated in loving memory to my father and my Grandma Eva—truth-seekers.

TABLE OF CONTENTS

Acknowledgements

So many people helped to make this book possible, including the following:

• All the mothers who have shared their stories with me over the years. Thank you for your trust, your time, and your honesty.
• Carol Wenzlau, the best mother-in-law and editor a writer could ask for. She is the grammar queen.
• My girlfriends: Lisa Horton, Darcy Spence, Jill Stevenson, Ellece Bill-Schmitz, and Denise Williams, and my swim buddies: Barbara Molloy, Kim Coontz, Claudia Greco, Karen Firestein, and Sharon Blaha. Thank you for all your encouragement.
• Anyone who asked me, "When are you going to finish that book?"
• Christine Fry. Your life and your writing have inspired me more than you will ever know.
• The members of the Valley/Foothill Doula Collective of Sacramento. You are an incredible group of giving women.
• Writers who aren't afraid to tell the truth about motherhood: Melissa Gayle West, Anne Lamott, Susan Straight, Shoshana Bennett, Vicki Iovine, and Sally Placksin among many.
• My extended family: Mom, Dean, Laurel, Derek, Leah, Deanna, Jackie, Sage, Aunt Mary, Uncle Bob, Nancy, Russ, Jim, Kari, Sam, Michael, Lynn, and Rich. I love you all.
• Cathy Dean, my life coach and editor. I would never have finished the book without your help. You are awesome!
• Angela Hoy and Julie Sartain. Thank you for being my publishing doulas.
• My amazing daughters, Danielle and Linda. Nothing I do in life will ever be as important as being your mom. You bring me so much joy, and I love you deeply.
• My husband, Mark. Thank you for supporting me no matter what crazy ideas I come up with. You are my best friend and the sweetest man on Earth. I love you with all my heart, and I look forward to being that old couple holding hands and walking through the park.

Introduction

It's 1:00 a.m. on our first night home from the hospital with our newborn daughter. My husband Mark and I are sitting on the floor in the nursery passing the baby back and forth. We are all crying. Mark and I are so tired we can hardly hold our heads up, but Danielle won't sleep. After a forty-six hour labor, an episiotomy, and difficulties getting my daughter to latch on for breastfeeding, I am a mess. All I can do is cry and wish for sleep.

In moments when I can muster a complete thought, one question burns in my brain—why didn't anyone tell me it could be like this?

* * *

While pregnant, I took all the classes my hospital offered and read dozens of books about preparing to have a baby. I didn't realize I also needed to learn about my own needs after the birth and to hear other women's stories about early motherhood.

During the first year of motherhood, I ached for those stories.

I now see my expectations about how I would handle motherhood were too high. I wasn't prepared for the physical and emotional upheavals in my body or for how taxing newborn care could be. I felt so incompetent because I couldn't make life run smoothly with a baby in the house. What was wrong with me?

I felt scared and overwhelmed too many times to count during those early months. I thought I had made a huge mistake by delivering this precious child into the world. I was sure I was a horrible mother. I cried often and many days wondered how I would last until Mark came home from work.

From hundreds of discussions with mothers, I've learned that my experiences were not unique. What's shocking is the secrecy that surrounds the difficulties young mothers face. Many are afraid that if they talk about how challenging motherhood can be, they will be judged harshly by their family, friends, or even strangers.

Doctors and childbirth educators sometimes gloss over the time after the baby is born and put all focus on the birth. Of course, the birth is incredibly important, but what about the weeks and months that follow?

I've found that being candid about the ups and downs of parenting leads mothers to sigh with relief and say, "Thank goodness. I thought I was the only one who felt that way."

I now work as a postpartum doula and help new families at home after they have a baby. My mission is to provide a safe place to talk about what new parenthood is truly like. I want to lift the veil of secrecy that surrounds the lives of postpartum women.

This book is filled with stories about the joys and sorrows of early motherhood. They include stories from a mom with breastfeeding difficulties, a mid-life mother, a woman whose baby couldn't leave the hospital, a teen mom, and many others. The final chapter profiles a woman who planned well and successfully managed the first months with her baby.

Whether you're expecting or already in the throes of newborn care, these women invite you into the sisterhood of mothers. If at times you find that being a mother is harder than you expected, you are not alone. Life with a baby can be chaotic, exhausting, thrilling, scary, joyous, and overwhelming—sometimes all in the same day! Let the lessons these women learned about what helps, and what doesn't, guide you through the rough spots. I hope you find knowledge, encouragement, and nurturing within these pages as you begin your parenting journey.

CHAPTER ONE

Sarah: "It's A Myth That Motherhood Is Instinctual"

When Sarah was eight weeks pregnant, she had an appointment with her midwife, Kathie. Kathie found that Sarah's uterus was bigger than it should be, so she suggested a routine ultrasound. After the ultrasound, Kathie told Sarah, "You have two babies."

"I felt the blood drain out of me and went totally numb," Sarah says. "I sent Kathie to get my husband, Andy. When he came in, I held up two fingers to tell him. Andy was elated. I was neutral. I didn't know twins growing up and they don't run in my or Andy's families. I'm still shocked at times that I had them."

During her pregnancy, Sarah found it difficult to field other people's reactions about the twins. "Everyone said, 'You poor thing. How are you going to handle it?' It was rare that someone would be positive. Andy and I role-played how to react to comments because my anxiety about it made the comments worse. I did have one girlfriend with twins who was very positive and who saw it as an amazing experience."

Most of Sarah's pregnancy was trouble-free, except for some bad edema (swelling) in her feet, but the added risks of carrying multiples was scary. "At one point I stopped reading stuff about the risks of them being premature...I just followed how I was feeling and trusted it. Emotionally I felt good—very prepared to be a mom and in a strong marriage."

Getting Ready for Twins

Once they knew about the twins, Sarah and Andy adjusted their postpartum plans. Sarah arranged to go back to work part-time rather than full-time, and they hired cleaning help and a postpartum doula (for a complete definition of postpartum doula, see the article, *Postpartum Doulas: Nurturing Help For Your Family*, in Appendix

B.) "I became fixated on having everything prepared. I really wanted things ready early in case of mobility issues. We moved my stepson Christopher's room and spent as much time getting his room prepared as the babies' room. We looked at the birthing center and visited the emergency room several times. I also researched support for twin moms on the internet."

Sarah found the Girlfriend's Guide books to both pregnancy and the first year to be helpful, as was the book, *Mothers of Multiples.* Jane Seymour's book, *Two At A Time,* however, she found "terrible." "Seymour said for example that the catering staff always made sure that she had a good diet provided at every meal. After the birth of her twins she talked about the round-the-clock nanny staff that she felt so great about. My feeling after reading the book was 'hmmm, how nice for her, the famous TV star, that everyone took great care of her.' I didn't feel as though it gave me much of a real-world perspective."

"Watching the Birth Day show on cable helped me prepare. The website zerotothree.com [a site dedicated to parents of infants and toddlers] had lots of developmental info.

"I think it would have helped if I had taken more time off before the birth instead of just two weeks. To have alone time to be quiet and still and wrap my mind around that I was having twins. It also would have helped if someone told me how all the attention shifts from you to the babies after birth."

By thirty-eight weeks, Sarah was having trouble staying comfortable. The edema was worse, she had lots of heartburn, wasn't sleeping well, and had an itchy rash across her stomach. She was also starting to worry if the babies were okay and considered having a cesarean section, although her doctor said it wasn't necessary.

Delivery

Sarah and her doctor decided she should come to the hospital to get induced so her labor would start. "We liked this particular doctor quite a bit and wanted her to do the delivery if possible. That's why we scheduled it for the day that she would be on call."

Sarah was administered Pitocin, a medication that is given intravenously and used to begin or increase the frequency of uterine contractions. Even with the Pitocin, "not much happened except for minor contractions," Sarah says. Seven hours later, the doctor upped the dosage of the Pitocin and then, around 9:00 p.m., broke Sarah's water. "Breaking the water was like flipping a switch. The contractions started coming harder. It was pretty hellish until midnight. We couldn't have a midwife there because I was having twins, and so they have you deliver in the emergency room. I have a fear of hospitals, so it helped that we had visited the emergency room so much."

"Would you believe that drugs (pain medication) actually didn't cross my mind? I went into the labor process with a very open mind, and I think that is perhaps the only bit of advice that you can really give someone. Of course, I thought it would be great if I actually could deliver my babies without drugs, but there are so many variables and so many unknowns that I really felt that it would be best to limit my expectations as much as possible. I think that when women or couples are dead-set on having drugs or not having drugs, it can be very disturbing when the inevitable 'labor curveball' is thrown. All of a sudden, there is a tremendous amount of fear or guilt about wanting or needing to go against the original plan.

"Seeing me in pain got to be too much for Andy. A nurse named Sandy was helpful. She told me, 'It's not going to get any worse than it is now.' That is exactly what I needed to hear. I thought I could survive what I was experiencing in that moment, but not an ounce more. Sandy also maintained good eye contact with me.

"I did finally ask for drugs, but they told me I was already dilated 9.75 centimeters. My doctor was scheduled to come back to the room at 12:30 a.m. to check me, and she was three minutes late. I was freaked out about those three minutes."

When it was time to push, Sarah experienced more severe pain. "I pushed for forty-five minutes. Finally the doctor said, 'Hold off for a minute and then you'll be able to see a head,' but Matty came out completely in the next push. Three more pushes and Joe

5

came out. I ended up with what's called a Level 3 tear—halfway to the back (rectum)." Both boys weighed over six pounds.

Afterwards, Sarah experienced uncontrollable shaking and some hemorrhaging, but she ended up being fine. She also didn't know until birth that she would be having two boys. During Sarah's pregnancy ultrasounds "there was general consensus that Baby A was a boy, but Baby B never seemed to show his hand. That's why we didn't know for sure. Believe me, we wanted to know...I had always thought I would have a girl; twin boys were last on the list. I was afraid I wouldn't get over that disappointment."

First Week

Andy stayed in the hospital with Sarah and the boys, but Sarah was nervous about when they would have to leave. "I didn't want to go home. I was so supported and cared for in the hospital. The day we were suppose to leave, the checkout process started sometime in the afternoon. I didn't realize that it would take so long. Both boys had to be seen by a pediatrician, and I had to be checked out. By the time we were getting ready to pack up, it was getting dark outside, and I panicked...I went into the bathroom to get my things and just broke down crying. I didn't want to go home in the dark. I really felt like I needed to go home in the morning when I could have a fresh start to the day—and my new life.

"Andy went out to the nurses station to explain our situation. I don't know if it was because we had twins, or because it was a slow night, but Sandy told us that of course we could stay another night and that she thought that was a better idea anyway.

"When I did go home the next day, I cried the whole way. The house looked so unfamiliar when we walked in—like I'd been away for months. What could be more life altering? You leave the house on a Thursday and come home after a long weekend on Monday morning with two tiny lives in your hands. You come home a different person. I was also disappointed that I still looked three months pregnant...However, I was relieved that the anticipated disappointment about not having a girl didn't happen.

"I didn't want people to come over, but Andy did. It seemed people stayed too long, and I felt overwhelmed. They helped, but I didn't know what to tell them to do. I had to let people help in the way they felt most comfortable. It was just easier that way. It was also hard to get a full break because, even when someone helped, I still had another baby to care for."

Life With Two Newborns

"I hadn't been around infants much, so I was unprepared for how small they were. Breastfeeding went fine, but I do feel that I didn't get a chance to enjoy it. I felt pressured because there were two. You don't instinctively know how to do it, and the babies don't either.

"I would feed two at a time. It was hard to get them to nurse at the same time though. I would wake the other one up when one was feeding. I had to keep a chart because I wouldn't remember when I had fed them last. I was impatient to have some semblance of a schedule since I was use to one.

"Andy and I would both get frustrated. He would turn to me for answers, but I wouldn't know what to do. It's a myth that motherhood is instinctual. I relied heavily on books like, *Secrets of the Baby Whisperer.*

"I would also take stuff personally, like when the babies cried. I felt like it was a reflection on me."

Dealing With New Mom Fatigue And Emotions

Exhaustion was a huge problem for Sarah, as it is with most new mothers, whether they have multiples or not. "I attribute most of the difficulties to exhaustion," she says. "I cried easily and just felt emotionally raw and vulnerable. I wasn't ever out of control, but I was hypersensitive. Also, I'm not a napper normally, so it was hard to catch up on sleep.

"Andy seemed to know when to do something extra for me—like breakfast in bed, a gift, a card, or flowers. He reassured me that I was doing an incredible job...I was very protective about seeing the babies in a positive light, even if it wasn't accurate. I wanted to see them as how I wanted them to be. I was sensitive to negative comments. "I don't know how people have babies without a partner or when they don't want the baby. I had the babies in the best of circumstances and still was overwhelmed and challenged. Sometimes I would go through the day and not shower or brush my teeth. You can't know until you're in it, but I still wonder—why didn't anyone tell me it's really hard and that it can be hellish? You run at such a sleep deficit that one good night doesn't do it."

Since Sarah was breastfeeding, Andy would sometimes sleep through a lot of what happened at night. "Andy is just about deaf in one ear. When his good ear is down on the pillow, he can't hear much. I wake up at the first sign of a whimper. Consequently, the boys could be crying, waiting to be latched on, and Andy wouldn't stir. My problem was that I didn't want to wake him up because he was still working. I felt that I should be able to handle it so he could get enough rest to function the next day." When Andy asked, "What's going on at night," it would lead to arguments. Sarah started keeping a nursing journal to help him understand what was happening through the night. Here's an entry from when the boys were a week old, showing when each baby was awake:

Joe - 8:30-8:45 p.m.
Joe - 9:40-10:00 p.m.
Matt - 11:18-11:28 p.m.
Joe - 11:55 p.m. - 12:07 a.m.
Matt - 12:39 a.m. - 12:50 a.m.
Joe - 1:30 a.m. - 1:52 a.m.
Matt - 2:28 a.m. - 2:47 a.m.
Joe - 3:38 a.m. - 3:48 a.m.
Matt - 4:24 a.m. - 4:52 a.m.
Joe - 5:05 a.m. - 5:15 a.m.
Matt - 5:15 a.m. - 5:30 a.m.

You can see that Sarah usually got less than an hour break between caring for a baby. "Finally I just started waking Andy up at night and ultimately that worked. He could lend the extra hands needed, but, more importantly, he could strategize with me about what to do."

New And Old Relationships

"My mom came for two weeks and then Andy's mom for a week. I wasn't use to spending so much time with family, so it drove me a little nuts. I needed space, but had to give that up some. Letting go of control was hard."

Sarah found a group of twin moms to walk with in her neighborhood once a week. "They knew how hard it was. It provided comfort and support that others had been through what I was going through." Sarah also received lots of positive reinforcement about how calm she was with the babies. "I just thought—what choice do I have?

"I really missed Andy. Even though you're living together, it's like you're apart. I missed having the time and energy to focus on our relationship and this incredible new bond we shared. Another relationship that changed was the one with my dad. He comes over two to three times a week now and we're closer. He's more involved in my life."

Struggles With Bottle Feeding

The babies started taking breastmilk from a bottle when they were just under a month old. They took to the bottles without any problems and that gave Sarah some relief since someone else could feed them.

"Once they're on the bottle though, don't take a break from it," she says. "During the holidays we went on vacation and I solely breastfed for two weeks. It then took over two months to get them back on the bottle." The boys would fuss or just not eat when others tried to give them a bottle during that time. Sarah worked with her doula and others to solve the problem. "We tried having me leave the house during feedings, walking around while feeding them, having the person feeding them hold the boys facing out so they wouldn't fuss that it wasn't me. I think we even poked extra holes in the nipples because they were not getting enough flow."

Things That Helped

Sarah was glad she had hired a postpartum doula in advance. "It was good to have someone totally neutral. I think it's good to look into hiring a doula while you are still pregnant. It can be a gift from your in-laws or other relatives. I would go out when the doula came over at times, and that was great, although, at first, strange. I would drive away alone, but felt lost thinking—what do I do? Where do I go?

"Someone holding a baby was a big help. Swaddling was also key for soothing them when they cried. The mobile over the boys' crib was good for entertaining them. I also remember how good taking a shower felt and not wanting to get out.

"4:00-6:00 p.m. was the hardest time of day. Both boys would be crying, and I would be at the end of my rope. I would be mad that Andy didn't come home sooner and told him he had to get home earlier. I just felt like a wreck. Then Andy would make a great dinner for us, and I'd feel better. We tried to have dinner together every night.

"People would tell me that this all would pass. It helped to remember it was a phase and things would get better. I felt like I was always trying to figure things out. No matter how tired you are, you still have to do it. Eliminate worrying about cleaning the house or have someone else do it or pay someone to do it. Delegate things out. Things won't get done the way you would do them, and that's okay. Don't redo something someone else has done. People don't feel like they're helping if you redo it, and they won't want to help again."

Sarah says that being a mother to twin boys is "the most incredible thing I've experienced...you don't know until you have them. It's the hardest thing I've ever done, the most relentless. But when they can give back the smallest thing, like a smile, it's worth it.

"Being a mom has challenged me in ways I couldn't have anticipated. My children require me to be more patient and more giving than I thought I could be. That's not to say that I achieve that every day, but I certainly am faced with challenges every day that push me to recognize where my strengths and weaknesses are. The experience is profound...no one has ever challenged me to grow and embody the person I know I can be more than they have."

AUTHOR'S REFLECTIONS

When Sarah found out she was expecting twins, she and Andy altered their postpartum plans. I advise my expectant clients to prepare as if they are having one more baby than they really are. If you're pregnant with one, prepare as if you're having twins. If pregnant with twins, plans as if triplets are on the way, and so on. I don't think I've ever heard a new mom say that she had too much help lined up. Having a partner who is a gourmet cook, like Andy, doesn't hurt either!

As Sarah pointed out about pain medication during labor, it can be detrimental to become too dependent on a certain outcome. It's good to know your options, but remain as flexible as you can with your expectations. This is true for all stages of parenting, but especially during the early years when you're adjusting to your new role as a mom.

Sarah also found that you have to enlist help at night to survive. In most cases, going to a full-time job away from the home is a lot easier than staying home with a baby, or babies in Sarah's case, so there's no reason not to have your partner help with nighttime care. Both parents participating during the night can make a huge difference in the mom's physical recovery and her mental state.

If you need extra help at night, it's more than worth it to budget for hiring a nighttime doula or baby nurse. They are worth their weight in gold.

CHAPTER TWO

Beth S.: "Breastfeeding Was Almost Like Poison For Me"

While pregnant, Beth never considered that she would have trouble breastfeeding. She didn't buy any baby bottles or learn how to prepare formula. "I had a very rigid view in my mind of what kind of mom I would be," she says. "I was going to fully breastfeed, use only cloth diapers, and be the cool mom. I'm sure those rigid images made my first weeks as a mother harder."

After a nineteen-hour labor, that included Pitocin and an epidural, Beth delivered her son, Eli, by cesarean section on August 6, 2002, at 11:15 p.m. "At the time I was too exhausted and doped up to realize, but the c-section was a really scary experience. I remember right after the birth, my husband, Nick, brought this little baby up to my face and, when I said, "Eli," he opened his eyes a little and gave me a sidelong glance. Later, when they wheeled me to my room around 3:00 a.m., I felt as tired as I'd ever been before."

Beth, Eli, and Nick stayed at the hospital for three days. During that time, Beth relied heavily on the nurses and lactation consultants on staff. They assisted her in getting Eli to latch on and gave Beth breaks from baby care. The first night in the hospital Eli woke up a lot and, out of desperation, Beth guiltily asked a nurse to take him out of the room. The nurse did and assured Beth, "Don't feel bad. That's what we're here for."

Things Get Worse At Home

When she was released from the hospital, Beth's world came crashing down. "My first days at home were scary and bad. I had bad postpartum depression and was anxious all the time. The first few days were a blur...I don't know how I survived them."

Beth felt trapped and wanted to get away. "It was different from what I expected because I had imagined that it was going to be the most over-the-top blissed out experience that I had ever had. Instead of a sweet little baby doll, I had a little lump that cried all the time. I felt like a dirty, sweaty pig who was exhausted and miserable and panicky. For the longest time, I saw no light at the end of the tunnel...I wondered, what the hell do I do with this baby? Those first weeks you're there to love them, but they give nothing back."

Beth adds, "I have never felt so isolated and helpless as I did when my son was born. I was actually scared of the baby. I didn't want to be left alone with him. I was so afraid that I would do something wrong, and he would end up getting hurt. I remember even thinking that I could put him up for adoption and tell my co-workers that he had died! I never wanted to hurt him. I just didn't think I was capable of taking care of him...I hadn't been around babies much since I'm an only child, and I was so unprepared for how hard and constant it is to be a mother."

Relationship Issues

Beth's mom came to help out for five days during the first week at home. Unfortunately, there was friction between Beth's mother and Nick, which often happens when relatives visit a family with a new baby. Beth and Nick have a small two-bedroom house. No one had much privacy, and sleep deprivation took a toll. "Emotions were definitely heightened," Beth says. "My mom was a help, but she had never breastfed and couldn't address my concerns about nursing. The tension between her and my husband was just another thing that fueled my anxiety and panic."

Due to an unexpected increase in his workload, Nick was pressured to return to work only six days after Eli's birth. All these stresses strained the marriage. "I remember we had one whopper of a fight (among many) during that time where I absolutely snapped," Beth says. "Nick had said, 'I don't know what you do all day. The house isn't clean.' I started screaming and slamming doors, and I told him that if he didn't start appreciating me I was going to leave him...I don't think he was prepared to see me so helpless and anxious.

"Since Nick went off to work every day, he didn't understand what I was going through...It's a myth that babies help a marriage. You have to negotiate time so that everyone gets a break. What did help was when Nick started spending whole days with Eli, and he could see how much work it was."
When Beth's mom left to go home, Beth felt "devastated. I kept asking myself—why can't I handle it? I was so overwhelmed with the house and the baby." Beth called a nurse about a local postpartum support group, but the group wasn't scheduled to meet again for three weeks. She cried on the phone to the nurse and wondered how to last until the meeting.

Breastfeeding Problems

On top of the anxiety and feelings of depression, breastfeeding had become a nightmare. "I hated breastfeeding, and it made me feel trapped. I hated the baby's constant need to be on my breast. The minute he was done nursing, he would get fussy and upset," she says. "I didn't have any pain, but I never leaked and never felt like I was producing enough. When I pumped, I would get maybe an ounce." Eli would squirm away or sometimes start to cry on the breast also. "I wanted out! I felt like breastfeeding was almost like poison for me."
Beth's friend, Carrie, a lactation consultant and pediatric nurse, would come over some days to help. She would show Beth different nursing positions and support her in getting Eli latched on. When Carrie wasn't there, though, Beth felt severe apprehension when Eli was getting hungry. "Breastfeeding caused me resentment toward the baby," she says. "I remember one time even saying to my mom, 'I hate him,' I was that miserable about nursing." Beth was also frustrated when breastfeeding organizations she contacted about her difficulties would tell her to "just keep trying and you'll get a good latch."
Around this time, Beth started taking Zoloft for her anxiety. "It's funny," she says. "I didn't want to admit that I had postpartum depression, but I would take Zoloft. I felt so despondent and

15

desperate. I would cry uncontrollably often." Beth's denial about her depression is not uncommon. The stigmas in American society about depression make it hard to admit you need help with a mental health problem.

Appetite And Weight Issues

Beth's anxiety was also affecting her appetite. She gagged or threw up every morning from stress over facing the day ahead. She says she would wake up and think—"oh no, here we go again." At two-weeks postpartum, she had lost an unhealthy twenty-nine of her thirty-nine pounds of baby weight.

Eli was having weight problems also. He had lost a pound since birth, which was normal for his size, but he wasn't gaining it back. After his two-week check-up, Beth breastfed around the clock for four days hoping that the baby's weight would increase. When she took him in for another weigh-in, he hadn't gained an ounce. "I felt like a failure, but I couldn't go on that way. Everyone was telling me to stop nursing: Nick, my doctor, Eli's doctor, my mom, my friends. After Eli's weigh in, I finally gave myself permission to stop.

"I remember when I first brought up trying bottles and formula to Nick, and he said it was fine. I was totally relieved." After Eli switched to formula feeding, there was a dramatic change in the baby. Beth says, "He slept better; his temperament was better. I was more relaxed. I truly felt elation when I finally decided to stop breastfeeding."

Trouble Finding Support

Shortly after Beth stopped nursing, she attended a new mom's support group. "The support group was a mistake that pushed me deeper into depression," she says. "I sat there for about two hours listening to everyone extol the superiority of breastfeeding. I was so freaked out that I had ruined my baby's chances for a normal life by deciding not to breastfeed. One mom I talked to privately said not to worry about the breastfeeding issue and that helped. But I still went home and sobbed uncontrollably."

In general, Beth found other new moms were afraid to speak the truth about what they were going through. "It only made me more anxious that they were together and knew what they were doing and were clean and pretty, while I was a disaster who didn't have a clue and needed a bath." Older moms and friends who told her that it was going to get better were the biggest help. She also wishes she hadn't let other's comments, like the ones at the support group, bother her so much. "People will make comments about your parenting forever," she says. "Take what's useful and ignore the rest. Do whatever works for you."

What Would Have Helped

In retrospect, Beth thinks it would have helped if someone had told her during pregnancy that the first six weeks postpartum have the potential to be REALLY hard. "Issues come up that you are not prepared for. I wish someone had told me that no matter how much I prepared, there were going to be things that would come up that would kick my ass...People always talk about lack of sleep, but there are so many other issues: anxiety, panic, wanting to escape, hating your husband, your baby, yourself. Harder things to talk about than, 'Oh, you'll be really tired.' While pregnant I had read books, magazines, and talked to lots of people about having a baby. None of those sources touched upon the emotional connection. I felt absolutely blind-sided by my emotions and the experience.

"I was shocked by how exhausted and sad I was. I longed for life before the baby. I knew life would change, but I thought I would still be really happy. I also was resentful that Nick got to go to work. At first, you get gifts and flowers, and people bring meals. Then, when that stops, you're like—now what? What you really need, for a lot longer than a week, is an extra pair of hands and someone to listen and encourage you. To say you're doing okay.

"What helped me the most was having a postpartum doula." Beth hired a doula when Eli was four weeks old. "I knew that someone was coming over at certain times who could help me. Someone who could reassure me that I was doing well, that Eli didn't have colic, and that I was not a complete idiot who was going to totally screw up her baby. It was great to have the adult contact. I think all new mothers should get help as soon as they need it.

"One day I came back from Target, and my doula showed me how to do the five S's method, and it was like magic. Eli stopped fussing right away and, if I remember correctly, fell asleep. It was a tactic Nick and I used for quite a while whenever we needed to calm him down." In order the five S's are: Swaddle the baby, hold him in a Side or Stomach lying position, Shush loudly in his ear, Swing him from side to side, and then give him something to Suck on. The method was developed by Dr. Harvey Karp, author of, *The Happiest Baby on the Block*.

Things started to improve when Eli was around seven weeks old. Beth felt intense relief that she was finally starting to bond with the baby. "I want new moms to know that they will be over the moon eventually, but nothing is wrong with them if they aren't over the moon with delight right away. They will come to love their babies more profoundly and more completely than they could have ever imagined. I remember in the first few weeks that I didn't really feel love for Eli. I just went through the motions of his care. With the accumulation of time and experience (and Eli's ability to smile and laugh), I fell in love with him, and now I can't get enough of him."

AUTHOR'S REFLECTIONS

The pressure Beth felt to breastfeed, and the shame she felt about quitting at three weeks after birth, are stresses that many new mothers experience. The majority of messages pregnant women hear are that you should only consider breastfeeding. Every expectant mother should be informed about the positive nutritional benefits of breastfeeding, but isn't it more important to support mothers no matter what feeding choice they make?

I had a horrible time breastfeeding my oldest daughter, Danielle. I experienced pain at every nursing and suffered from cracked, bleeding nipples. I don't know if Danielle was ever latched on correctly and, by the time she was six weeks old, I quit breastfeeding because I couldn't handle the pain anymore. No one had told me about lactation consultants (this was in 1992), and there was not a local chapter of La Leche League, an organization that helps women breastfeed. Nothing in my pregnancy reading had stated that I might have difficulty nursing. Additionally, I was uncomfortable breastfeeding in public because I leaked so much. So breastfeeding made me more housebound than a mother who could nurse away from home.

I still feel guilty that I wasn't able to nurse Danielle longer. When I quit nursing, I felt incredible relief to be done with it, yet shame at my failure. I worked so hard to breastfeed successfully, but it just wasn't meant to be for me at that time.

Excessive pressure about breastfeeding does not help new mothers. What does help is educating them about how to nurse and providing them with information like the phone numbers of lactation consultants, breastfeeding support lines, and stores that sell breastfeeding supplies. (For breastfeeding resources, see Appendix A.) If breastfeeding doesn't work for them, they shouldn't be chastised, but respected for doing the best they can.

CHAPTER THREE

Amy: "I Didn't Think Past Delivery"

L ike so many women, Amy had preconceived notions about how she would handle becoming a mother. "I thought three things about motherhood: that I would do it, would do it well, and would be happy while I was doing it," she says. "Once I had Xavier, I couldn't understand why things that worked for other mothers, didn't work for me."

In January of 2003 Amy miscarried her first pregnancy at thirteen weeks. While taking the fertility drug, Clomid, she conceived again in April. "I was so afraid—certain, really—that a miscarriage would happen again. Even after Xavier was far enough along that he could live if he had to be taken out early, I still was certain he wasn't going to make it...that did add a lot of stress which showed itself in worry and heart palpitations.

"I was consumed by pregnancy," she says. Despite her worries about the baby's health, Amy found pregnancy "fun." "People ask you about your doctor's appointments and how you feel. I didn't think past delivery...I read lots of things about pregnancy and preparation for birth, but I did not read anything—NOTHING—about newborns and their care...We did take a six-week childbirth class, and the nurse instructor showed us a few things like bathing a baby and caring for a circumcision...A different nurse taught us the breastfeeding stuff, and she talked about inverted and flat nipples. She offered to look at our breasts to see if they were okay or not for breastfeeding, but I just felt too weird!

"I did do some practical things, like brown hamburger meat and freeze it into meal-sized portions so I'd have an easy base for suppers like spaghetti. Our family and friends gave us three baby showers, so we had lots of stuff, and I had washed it all, organized it, and set up everything...We had lots of equipment and clothes. But no breastfeeding stuff—no nursing pads or bras, no pump, no 'know-how.'"

Baby Comes Early

Amy was due January 1, 2004, but woke up at 5:00 a.m. on December 20, 2003, because she "felt a little weird." Thirty minutes later her water broke. She called her midwife, Mary. "We go to the women's clinic in a town an hour-and-a-half away so Mary said we should head up to the hospital. I said I wanted to do the first part of labor at home, because that's what the Bradley childbirth method encourages, so I took a shower, and my husband, Brandon, walked our dog. I shaved my legs and curled my hair...We were caught off guard because the baby was coming early, so we weren't packed."

Amy's labor escalated quickly. "I was surprised and afraid by 8:00 a.m. and did not want to leave the toilet because every time I had a contraction I would leak some fluid. We finally got in the car and made it to the hospital...When we got there, I felt the need to push already, but I was only dilated four centimeters.

"I labored for two hours in the hospital, then pushed for an hour. I was a bad pusher. It hurt so much. I just didn't know how to do it. I tried to push with my legs instead of with my stomach muscles. I had been practicing squatting and had really hoped to push in that position, but Mary didn't want me to do that, so I had to lie down with my legs in stirrups. It was awful...I remember my skin hurting on my shoulders and arms and my eyes feeling like they were going to pop out. I really don't think labor was that bad, but pushing was hell." Xavier was born at 12:38 p.m.

"I didn't hold Xavier until he was forty-five minutes old. They were cleaning him up, and I was frustrated with that. Also, he was born on a Saturday, and there is no lactation consultant on the weekends." The nurses were somewhat abrupt and asked Amy, "Do you want to nurse him or not?" "I didn't know to try to nurse him," she says. "When I did, I thought he would snuggle with the breast. I didn't know how often to nurse or anything."

First Weeks

Monday evening, the family went home. Brandon took two weeks off from work, but, Amy says, "Neither of us knew anything...Our first days at home were awful. Xavier cried nonstop, and we did not know what to do...He flailed his arms so much that I could barely hold him to me to breastfeed."

Brandon would hold Xavier's arms down when Amy nursed him. "Xavier didn't know how to latch on and couldn't because of my flat nipples. He wouldn't open his mouth and would suck at the end of the breast. Then he would get mad and wiggly. I was scared he had a neurological disorder the way his arms flailed. It was Christmas time, and we were so tired and overwhelmed...Being a mom was all I'd ever wanted in my whole life, and I felt like I was failing at every turn."

"We had to have home health care come for about the first week since Xavier was jaundiced. They would try to help me some with the breastfeeding, and one of the nurses was really compassionate...She sold me her double electric pump for only $25 with all her bottles and accessories. She gave me nipple shields that helped the nipples stick out further. I also tried nipple shells when Xavier was five or six days old, and they helped.

"I was really mad and frustrated about the breastfeeding. Xavier cried and came off the breast all the time...If you don't decide that you'll do whatever it takes to breastfeed, then you'll give up. I was determined to make it work, but the first four months of nursing were pure torture."

The Realities Of Baby Care

For Christmas Eve and Christmas Day, the family went to Amy's parents' who live in the same town. Amy tried to rest, but "I kept hearing the baby screaming in my head (even though my mom was handling Xavier fine.) I couldn't sleep. I was quite the insomniac for many months. Even if Xavier was finally asleep, I couldn't relax and sleep."

Amy realized that her pre-birth notions about parenthood were far from accurate. "I thought caring for a baby was buying cute little outfits and taking the baby out. I just thought it was going to be fun. I didn't know what to do with him, like when I went to the bathroom. I didn't know how to use the baby equipment either. There were also lots and lots of days when Xavier didn't take a nap. "Some of my friends did bring meals the first week, and it was helpful. What I needed was sleep and someone to commiserate, not offer advice. Someone who would just sit around and let me cry or whatever. I would be honest with some women about the hard time I was having, but then they would give advice and that was almost worse...It would have helped if someone had said, 'It will not be like this forever.' I thought I would ruin Xavier if things didn't go right. I thought every little mistake and the crying and sleep issues were going to last forever."

Some Advice Helps, Some Doesn't

When Xavier was three weeks old, Amy's friend, Jennifer, came over. "She suggested that Xavier needed to have some time in a seat by himself to look around or play or fall asleep. I didn't know that! She spent the whole afternoon with us and offered a few pointers on breastfeeding and was just some company for me."

Around the same time another friend of Amy's suggested she try to put Xavier on a three hour feeding schedule and try the E.A.S.Y. (Eating, Activity, Sleep, You) method from the book, *Secrets of the Baby Whisperer*, by Tracy Hogg.

Amy's journal entry to Xavier from January 7, 2004 outlines her frustration when others suggestions didn't work: "Yesterday I got really worked up because I am so confused about what you want. Angie is big on the three-hour schedule, and everyone else keeps telling me you need awake time after you eat, but, if you don't fall asleep at the breast, you don't go to sleep! You just cry and cry. So I don't know what to do. I had a really bad day yesterday. I just don't know how to read your cries and your cues. I don't know what you are telling me! I'm trying! Today is going a bit better, but I still don't know how to tell what you are saying. Why can't I tell when you are tired or hungry? I try all the wrong things. I'm sorry."

As Amy further explains, "With the E.A.S.Y. method, I never got to the Sleep and the You. I couldn't understand why it didn't work for me like it had for my friend. I had no confidence in myself."

Dealing with colic and relationship issues

It became clear that Xavier suffered from colic (defined as three hours of crying per day, three days a week or more, for three weeks or more.) Xavier would hunch over when he cried, and his stomach would be rock hard. The first doctor Amy talked to about the colic—a general practitioner—said to just let Xavier cry for "a couple of hours" if needed. Amy dropped that doctor. She then went to a pediatrician who suggested Mylicon drops. "I don't think the drops helped," Amy says. "Xavier did like to be held facing out and liked lotion being put on his legs. Big dance movements with loud music helped. I would play Shania Twain or something with lots of drums and dance with him." The colic lasted fourteen long weeks.

On January 23rd, when Xavier was just over a month old, Amy wrote in her journal: "I feel like everyone can calm you better than I can. Is it because you think whenever I have you, you should eat? It's frustrating. I'm the momma. I should know how to help you! And it's nerve-wracking when we go somewhere because I'm so afraid you will cry, and I won't be able to make you stop."

Although Amy's parents live in the same town, her mom didn't offer to help much. "I know my mother was trying really hard not to interfere, but I really needed some help. She didn't breastfeed and says my sister and I were 'perfect babies,' so she was really confounded by our difficulties with Xavier. She told me, 'I just don't remember it being this hard.'... I think we both didn't know how to be a mother and daughter when the daughter becomes a mother. I know she would have helped me, done anything I asked her to, if only I had known what I needed to ask for. I was just surprised, I guess, that she didn't anticipate my needs (having been through it herself) and just DO things without my asking. Then again, I didn't want to admit that

I needed help. I felt like everyone else gets through it, so why can't I?"

Brandon and Amy had been married five years when they had Xavier. "We were always in sync on everything before...It was the first time that Brandon couldn't understand what I was going through. I tell him everything, and he is wonderful, a patient listener, but his experience with the baby was so different from mine. So then I was upset because he didn't get it."

Stress, Insomnia, And Depression

Since Xavier wasn't napping and was colicky, Amy became extremely physically and emotionally drained. She also couldn't sleep when she needed to. "I was afraid Xavier would get up and couldn't relax enough to sleep. Sometimes, I would fall asleep when he was nursing. I would also call Brandon at work during the day crying because I was so tired. When Brandon got home in the evening, I would lay down from 6:00 p.m. to 7:00 p.m., and Brandon would put Xavier to bed. I would be frantic if I wasn't ready to go to bed when he put the baby down since I knew then I would get sleep. We would trade off during the night caring for Xavier. I never tried to see if Xavier would go to sleep on his own because of the crying, and I think that was a mistake.

"I think I did have postpartum depression. At my six-week check-up, Mary offered me antidepressants, but I refused. I didn't want it to affect me or Xavier. I never took anything into my body during pregnancy more than Tylenol.

"I would talk to Brandon a lot, and he listened and hugged me and let me cry and didn't try to fix it. There are also some moms from my church that I can talk to...I would say the worst of it lasted until around three months and then gradually lessened from there."

Xavier's cord stump didn't fall off until he was five weeks old—on average, the stump falls off by two weeks—and that was another source of stress. "I could get worked up about things," Amy says. "It wasn't necessary, just upped my stress. I was afraid to do things unless other people had suggested them. I wish that I would have known that I could do whatever works, regardless of its weirdness.

Another of Amy's journal entries to Xavier dated March 15, 2004: "You are still very fussy a lot of the time. I feel so sad so much of the time because I don't know what you need or want. Saturday was awful—you cried pretty much nonstop from 2:00 p.m. until you finally went to bed at 10:30 or whenever it was. Sunday was a little better, but still lots of fussing and crying. Why are you so unhappy?"

From her experience, Amy advises new moms, "Don't be so hard on yourself! Don't worry about a schedule. Xavier set himself to a schedule when he was ready. I finally wised up and stopped listening to everyone's advice and just did what I thought felt right and then things went a lot more smoothly. The colic slowly went down, and I could distract Xavier better.

"Also, learn about breastfeeding and how to do it and buy the right supplies. Breastfeeding problems can snowball with your hormones, and you can get overwhelmed."

What Helped

"Making time for regular Bible study and prayer helped a lot. I needed to connect with my real source of power to get through the times that were so hard...I would pray to God for Xavier to sleep, but I'd be in tears. But I would be less alone because He was listening and was there. If I started my day with prayer or Bible study, my day would be a lot calmer. I'd feel more connected.

"I don't want to watch TV much, but food and home shows helped. By 4:00 p.m., I would feel crazy, like I would die. That time of day is hard because you feel like the day has been going on forever, so find ways to make the time better. A cooking show was on then, and I would reward myself by watching it. Shows like "Clean Sweep" on TLC where they go in and organize a messy house I also enjoyed because it worked out nice. I couldn't get out much for walks because it was winter, and the weather was bad, but new moms should get out to walk if they can. Talking to someone on the phone also helps.

"It took eleven months, but Xavier can take naps now and often sleeps from around 8:00 p.m. to around 5:00 a.m. and goes back to sleep for another hour or more after nursing. Some nights, he still gets up a couple of times a night, but we are doing so much better. Nursing has long since smoothed out too, and now I don't want to give it up! Just know that things change all the time with a baby, and that you are normal and okay."

AUTHOR'S REFLECTIONS

Jane Honikman, of Postpartum Support International, suggests that we are biologically predisposed while pregnant not to think beyond the birth. A hundred years ago, many women died in childbirth or, if they survived, family and community members took care of them during the early months. Those women didn't have to think about their own postpartum care. Our brains, unfortunately, have not caught up to the fact that in modern society, we don't have the new mom support of old. You have to plan for your own nurturing, which includes breaks from baby care. With breaks, you will be a better mother to your child. A mother's sleep deprivation, stress, and anxiety do not help anyone in the family.

The magic question is—how do we get pregnant women to think about their postpartum needs? I remember with my first pregnancy thinking that if I could just make it past delivery, everything else would be smooth sailing. I was so wrong. Like Amy, I too had a hard time asking for help when I was struggling with the exhaustion that comes with caring for a newborn. I wish I had put my pride aside and asked for the help I needed. Now if I could just get other moms to think past the birth, I'll have found the key to the kingdom!

CHAPTER FOUR

Marie: "I Broke Down In Tears Constantly"

At age thirty-nine, after deciding years earlier not to have children, Marie found herself pregnant. "My doctor had taken me off the Pill to check my thyroid and other issues," she says. "I thought I didn't need birth control for awhile, but, within a month, I was pregnant."

Marie and her husband, Ron, who have been together since high school, had always thought they couldn't settle down enough to have kids. "It had been just the two of us for so long. We went from being thrilled and excited half of the time (during the pregnancy) to absolutely terrified the other half of the time. It felt like one emotional extreme to the next. When I wasn't focused on how lousy I felt physically, I was able to be more excited about being pregnant."

Problems During Pregnancy

Eight weeks into her pregnancy, Marie started hemorrhaging and thought she had miscarried. When she went to the doctor, she found out she was still pregnant. The doctors could never confirm it, but she may have miscarried a twin.

During the fifth month of her pregnancy, she started to experience other physical problems. Marie had a lot of pressure in her lower groin and sleeping difficulties. Then, in the eighth month, panic attacks began occurring. "Before my pregnancy, I had only experienced some minor panic attacks right after the Northridge Earthquake [which occurred near Los Angeles in January of 1994.] The first panic attacks during pregnancy felt as though I couldn't breathe, and that I was spinning into a whirlpool-like hole, losing control. A very terrifying feeling of having to hold onto something solid like a countertop because, if I didn't, I would be sucked into this black hole. I really felt like I was totally losing control of my mind's ability to think rationally."

Marie also developed severe sinus problems. She remembers her ninth month of pregnancy as living in a complete state of panic. "Between the physical problems and my emotional ups and downs over becoming a mother after years of deciding not to have children, it was a tough time."

Marie took a childbirth preparation class and a baby care class, but was too sick to attend her breastfeeding class. She found the classes only briefly touched upon the emotional aspects of pregnancy and postpartum and that she was thirsting for more information. "I read *What to Expect When You're Expecting* over and over—so did my husband—and we talked and planned a lot. I'm an aunt, but really didn't have much hands-on experience with babies."

When her due date was nearing, the doctors discovered that the baby was breech, and they couldn't get him to turn. Marie was scheduled for a cesarean section on her due date, which was perfect timing because her water broke that morning. "They tried to give me an epidural, but it wouldn't take. I had to wait twenty minutes on the operating table before they could try the needle again. That was really scary. I was afraid I would have a panic attack." The second epidural did take, and Marie felt no pain during the c-section. Her son, Max, was born on March 19, 2001.

First Few Days

Her four days in the hospital were awful. "My room was so claustrophobic and stuffy," Marie says. "There were no windows, and I suffered severe panic attacks. I wasn't able to sleep. I would get up in the middle of the night and beg the nurses to come talk to me. The nurses and doctors were wonderful, but I felt completely alone. Max was in the room with me, but it's hard to remember him, even though I knew I would freak out if he was out of the room."

Marie was given Vicodin for her incision pain from the c-section and started on powerful anti-anxiety medication for the panic attacks. Because of all the medication, she wasn't able to breastfeed Max. She did pump her milk, but would have to dump it because of the medications in her system.

Anxiety Attacks Intensify

When she came home from the hospital, Marie's anxiety attacks became "full-blown." "The attacks that I had then were much more severe and difficult to think through," she says. Along with still feeling like she was sinking into a hole during the attacks, she also experienced shaking, dry mouth, and dizziness. "At no time did I ever feel like I was going to die, contrary to many others who have panic attacks. I just always felt as though I was going to go insane and be trapped in this dark hole where there was only fear and overwhelming anxiety, and that I would never be able to climb out again...I definitely think hormones made the attacks worse once Max was born."

Marie's mom came on the morning of their first day home and then went back to her own house in the afternoon. When Ron went out to the store later, Marie had a major panic attack. She called her mom on the telephone and asked her to come back. "The first days were an awful, painful, scary blur. My mom came a lot to help, but my husband really took the reins and did everything, because I was unable to function. I did breastfeed some because I was taking less medication and was told it was safe, but soon my breastfeeding was interrupted for several months when I had an ear infection and sinus problems and had to take antibiotics."

Marie was shocked by what was going on in her body. "My sheer exhaustion and inability to function, due to both the c-section recovery and the hormonal shifts, was the most surprising part for me. I had no idea the human body could take so much!" she says.

Confusion And Guilt About Motherhood

Marie felt completely disassociated from the baby during this time. She remembers looking at him across the room and thinking— oh, there's Max; there's a baby. She felt shame and anger at herself because she wasn't doting on him, like you see mothers do in the movies. "I truly felt as though I was going insane on many occasions and had no one to talk to who understood. No one had told me this might happen, so it threw me for such a loop."

She wishes she had been prepared for the possibility of hormonal and mood problems so she could have taken medication or joined a support group ahead of time. Since depression runs in her family, she also wishes a doctor had gone over her history and let her know that there was a good chance that she could have problems postpartum. She may have been suffering from postpartum psychosis, but a definite diagnosis was never made.

"I could not eat, sleep, or take medications at times for fear they would kill me. I did not want anything to do with the baby. I couldn't think. I broke down in tears constantly and dreaded the oncoming night. I was also afraid to go to sleep because I was afraid I would never wake up."

Marie did have occasional moments of clarity and joy when she had physical contact with Max, like when changing his diaper. "The present moment awareness would make me relax, but then I would slip back into panic mode."

She noticed that how ill she felt depended on the time of day. "The mornings were bad. Noon was good. Then, starting around 4:00 p.m., I would start feeling bad and go downhill from there. I could actually feel the shifts occurring throughout the day. My doctors told me, and I had read in several books on health and hormones, that around 4:00 p.m. my physical body was at its lowest energy level. I was able to start planning to do things before that time set in, like going outside or phoning a friend."

A Tough Recovery

What Marie and her doctors thought were sinus problems started causing severe pain between Marie's eyes. The doctors kept prescribing antibiotics, but the pain didn't go away. MRIs (magnetic resonance imagings) found nothing wrong. The recovery from her c-section was also much more painful than she had anticipated. There was a lot of pain and itching at the incision site. "It felt like a rope across my stomach, pulled tight," she says. "I don't know how women look like they are functioning after a c-section...Also, being an older mom made the physical recovery more difficult, which the doctors tend to blow over."

Sleeping continued to be difficult. "I was afraid if I slept too deeply, I wouldn't come out. I remember my mom feeling so bad because I told her I couldn't go to sleep unless she held me because I was so scared. I was so afraid that if I lost control, I would die." Marie agreed to take Sonata, a sleep aid, around three-weeks postpartum. "I asked my mom to watch Max, and Ron stayed in the room with me. I thought if enough people were there, I wouldn't go too deep. I slept for four hours straight [something that hadn't happened since before Max's birth], and it felt so good. I continued to take the Sonata for seven nights."

Marie would go for days at a time without eating during the postpartum weeks, and often gagged. "I would see food and want to vomit. I had to force food down. What helped was talking to somebody about how I was feeling. Sometimes after I got off the phone with a friend, I could eat. Otherwise, I had no appetite."

Although Marie is a practicing minister, she felt no connection to a higher power during the months after Max's birth. "I was operating on such a mental and physical level. There was no room for spirituality. I didn't pray or ask God for help because I was too caught up in physically getting through the day. I was spiritually and intellectually shut down."

Relationship Strains

Although Ron was Marie's biggest source of support, their relationship was strained some during this time. He rarely left Marie alone, and the stress of her depression wore on him. At two-months postpartum, she could tell that Ron was tired of her not doing well. "I was constantly asking Ron, 'Do you think I'll get better?' Nothing he could say or do would make me stop asking."

Other family members struggled with what Marie was going through. "They couldn't understand and didn't know what to say. I could feel their frustration. My sister, Angela, so badly wanted to help, but didn't know what to do. She did insist I call her friend who had suffered from anxiety issues. I was able to share stories with her friend, particularly about exhaustion issues."

What Helped

Marie turned to the internet and found it to be a lifesaver. She searched under Postpartum Depression Support Groups and found help at various discussion boards. A website that was particularly helpful to her was babycenter.com because "it offers tons of informative articles and message boards where you can get personal insight and ideas from other moms who have 'been there, done that.'" She did track down a local support group, but couldn't bring herself to go to the meetings because "when I would go out, I would panic. Everything looked too bright, nothing looked right." She also was able to call her local university's drug hotline and get questions answered about medications.

"Talking, talking, talking to anyone who would listen helped," she says. "I called every woman I ever knew who had a kid and talked their ears off." Marie suggests new mothers get on the internet, call their doctor, and go to a support group, if they can, or else have someone who checks in on them regularly. She also warns that you have to be careful to avoid people who make you feel worse. "But I also remember hearing other women's horror stories and realizing that I was not alone, and that they had gotten through it alive and okay, and so would I. I felt guilty and awful that I was not being the perfect mom, like I was damaged or something, until I learned more and more that my experiences were actually common. People kept saying that it would get better. I didn't believe it at first, but I hung onto it.

"The parameters for depression are so wide. There are many, many things you could experience as postpartum depression, but it can be treated, and it's common. Women need to know that they should get help when they are having depressive thoughts...It was truly a horrifying experience that NO ONE EVER TALKED ABOUT, not even my doctors...It pains me that women are still so in the dark about the difficulties of postpartum periods with or without depression.

"Getting out in the fresh air helped me, as did finally listening to my doctors and taking my meds [Marie started taking Zoloft around four-months postpartum.]" She advises, "Find time for yourself to read or meditate or even take a walk. For me, the best medicine was to get as educated as I could about what was happening to me so I could be in a position of power in trying to take control of my life back. I also wish I had done more silly stuff like watched more funny TV shows or movies. When I did watch shows like, 'I Love Lucy' or 'The Beverly Hillbillies,' it helped."

Older Mother Issues

Marie feels motherhood was harder physically because of her age and added to her lack of energy. "Health is the biggest issue. You're worried that your baby will have problems (like Down's syndrome) because of your age. You also wonder—will I live long enough to see my baby married and to see my grandkids? When the baby's twenty, I'll be sixty! It helped to read about other women in their forties who were having babies and also see shows like an episode of 'Oprah' that addressed older moms.

"The transition to motherhood is harder I think for older moms. You're use to being an individual with a developed career. On the positive side though, you are wise, and you know what you want."

Things slowly improved during Marie's third and fourth months postpartum. She started eating better and was getting more snippets of sleep. She has a clear memory of a day when Max was four months old, and she was driving him to the doctor. "The Modern English song, *I'll Stop the World and Melt With You*, was playing on the radio, and the sun was shining in a certain way," she says. "It hit me at that moment that I was going to be okay. I felt like the fog had cleared, and the pain between my eyes stopped. I felt so good. When you're in it, it doesn't feel like it's ever going to pass, but it does." When Max was five months olds, Marie was also able to resume breastfeeding and did so successfully for over a year.

"I'm so surprised at the resiliency and strength of women," she adds. "It's unbelievable that we're asked to go through so much to have a baby...So be prepared, reach out to others, and do not be afraid to get help right away...Also, realize it's hormonal, and you are not going insane. You are not alone. So many women go through this, and we need each other."

AUTHOR'S REFLECTIONS

Panic attacks are scary enough without having a baby to take care of at the same time. Luckily Marie had help from her husband and others, but what about women who don't have any help? Don't hesitate to call your doctor if you have symptoms like Marie's or the ones described below. You don't need to suffer with these symptoms.

Panic disorders occur in about ten percent of postpartum women. From the Postpartum Support International website, here are some facts about the disorder:

Symptoms

• Episodes of extreme anxiety
• Shortness of breath, chest pain, sensations of choking or smothering, dizziness
• Hot or cold flashes, trembling, palpitations, numbness or tingling sensations
• Restlessness, agitation, or irritability
• During an attack, the woman may fear she is going crazy, dying, or losing control
• Panic attack may wake her up
• Often no identifiable trigger for panic
• Excessive worry or fears (including fear of more panic attacks)

Risk factors

• Personal or family history of anxiety or panic disorder
• Thyroid dysfunction

Marie continued to look for help, which aided her recovery. Many women suffer alone in their homes, afraid of criticism by others if they tell the truth about what a hard time they are having. Instead of judging, we should educate doctors, families, and friends on how to help and encourage new mothers. When mothers have the support they need, they are less likely to experience maternal exhaustion and anxiety or to commit child abuse.

Education during pregnancy about postpartum emotional difficulties would have helped Marie prepare for the upheavals she might encounter. Regular check-ins with new mothers after the birth also could aid in catching problems before they worsen. Most women receive a six-week postpartum medical check-up, which may not include any evaluation of their mental state, and then they are left on their own to navigate the often rocky terrain of early motherhood. Babies have numerous well-baby check-ups. Why aren't there well-mother check-ups throughout the postpartum year?

CHAPTER FIVE

Kendra: "I Always Got Caught Up In The Moment"

When Kendra, age sixteen, told her mother that she was pregnant, "My mom said, 'Having the baby won't be good for you. You won't finish school. You'll depend on the government.'" Kendra's parents are divorced. Her mother suggested Kendra call her father and ask for money for an abortion. "My dad didn't believe in it [abortion], and didn't want that on his conscience. I didn't have money for an abortion, so then my mom said I should give the baby up for adoption. I couldn't do that. I knew if I did, then I would think about that baby all the time. I would rather have an abortion before I would give up my child...I think adoption is a great thing, but I just don't think it's right for me."

Kendra and her boyfriend Chris, who is nineteen, had been together on and off for five years when Kendra found out she was pregnant. "Chris is the only person I've had sex with," Kendra says. "We rarely used birth control. I just didn't care...I knew about condoms and I had asked my mom about birth control pills. She just said that I shouldn't be having sex...Chris and I just thought in the moment, not in the long run.

"I did get pregnant once before, but I had a miscarriage. I prayed to God then that if he would take that baby, I would never have unprotected sex again and, if I did, He could 'let' me get pregnant. And that's just what happened...I wasn't really worried about it [pregnancy] until after each time we had sex. Then I was like, okay, I'll never do that again. But I always got caught up in the moment."

Chris has a child with another woman that was conceived during a time when he and Kendra were broken up. That child was born in November of 2003, but the mother is neglectful. Chris and his parents (who he lives with) care for the baby.

During Kendra's pregnancy, Chris asked her to marry him. Kendra did want to marry Chris in the future, but "I didn't want it to get married now just because we have a baby. I wanted it to be because we love each other and the almost six years we've been together."

Family Conflicts

Kendra's baby was due in December of 2004. The summer before the birth, Kendra went to stay with her older sister. Her sister lives in a town three hours away. Kendra visits there most weekends and during school breaks because Chris and many of her relatives live in that town.

"I worked in day care that summer and didn't spend any money on myself. All the money went for the baby. One day I called my mom, and she said that I couldn't come back home. I cried so bad. I didn't talk to her again for a week. Then she said she was sorry, and it was okay to come home, so I did in August.

"My family didn't have anything nice to say to me at all [about the pregnancy.] They made me feel the worst I'd ever felt in my life. I didn't think they would act like that. It went on for five months. I never felt so depressed before. I have older twin brothers, and they were mad at me. They would say things like, 'You're stupid and irresponsible.'... I felt like I would be a terrible mother. I thought I would become another young, single mother on welfare...Everyone pumped my head up that it wasn't going to be right and that I wasn't mature enough and that I couldn't take care of the baby.

"Chris gave me money for the baby, and his mom was excited...The only people who comforted me at the start of my pregnancy were Chris' family and my cousins, Angie and Jasmine. I felt like I had no one else but Chris and my cousins on my side."

Mixed Feelings About The Pregnancy

In the fall, Kendra didn't return to school. "I was ashamed to go back...I didn't want to go out and associate with people. I didn't want to go to church. I mostly stayed in the house and babysat my niece. Friends did come over some. When I would go out, strangers would say things like, 'How old are you?' and would look over at me. It seemed so terrible that I was pregnant."

When she was six-months pregnant, Kendra's family started to accept the pregnancy. But she still had lots of doubts about keeping the baby. "I went to the library and checked out books on adoption. There were different stories saying it was the best thing for the baby, similar to what my family had been telling me. I wondered if maybe I should give him up so he could be raised in a two-person household. I called an adoption agency and asked a lot of questions.

"Nighttime was the most vulnerable time for me to feel bad. I called Chris one night and said, 'Would you be willing to sign over your rights for adoption?' He hung up on me. Chris later said, 'I'm not going to sign it, just give the baby to me.' I decided not to do it [adoption] and finally could say with conviction what my decision was."

To get ready for the baby, Kendra cleaned and washed all the baby items she had bought. "I took down all my posters and Furby toys. I cleaned all my walls and my whole room."

Cayden's Birth

Kendra went in for a doctor's appointment the morning of December third. "I didn't know I was in active labor until I went to my doctor. They said I was dilated three centimeters and that I was ready to get a room. That was around eight or nine a.m....The contractions started coming closer together. At noon, they gave me Pitocin because my labor had slowed down and then an epidural at 3:00 p.m. Cayden was born at 8:55 p.m. My mom, Tasha (my sister-in-law), and a family friend were with me...I guess I have a high tolerance for pain because I didn't scream or anything during the labor.

"When I first saw Cayden, I cried because I had so much love for him. And because of everything I gave up just to keep him. One of the nurses said she had never seen that much love in a teen mother's eyes before...I decided maybe I can be a good mother and overcome the odds.

"I had good treatment in the hospital. The nurses treated me like an adult and were really nice. They gave me everything I asked for. I was sore some, but felt fine.

"I didn't breastfeed because I didn't think I could...I knew I would be too busy to pump milk, and I didn't want those swollen boobs...I think if I was a stay-at-home mom, I still would feel like that...I also wanted to eat a lot of junk food. I still wanted to be kind of a kid and not have to worry about eating right."

Dealing With Crying And Lack Of Sleep

Kendra and Cayden went home two days later on the fifth. "Our first day home was okay. I had my mom there to help me through everything the first week...My milk came in on December sixth. The pain was excruciating. It felt like sharp needles. When I touched my breasts, it made them leak. My mom told me to put cabbage leaves on them and that helped—it made it feel like dull needles instead of sharp ones. The leaves drew all the milk out. By the seventh, I was much better, but my milk coming in was worse than my labor.

"I was surprised about how much I had to do for Cayden every day. I thought I would feed him, change him, and he would go to sleep. That's not how it was. He didn't sleep a lot, and sometimes I would have to pat him for thirty minutes before he would even burp. I also didn't think he would go though all those clothes in one day. He would pee all over himself, and I would have to give him a bath and change his clothes.

"Cayden was a big crybaby, so I had to hold him all the time. I sometimes would have to lay him down and walk out of the room, breathe, count to ten, and get some water. I had to take every day one day at a time.

"He would nap for about two hours in the morning and then stay up for most of the day, only taking short cat naps. That's why I needed No Doz [an over-the-counter medication] to stay awake...Swaddling would help him to go to sleep, but he wouldn't sleep on his back. I was nervous about laying him on his stomach, but it was the only way to get him to sleep.

"After a week, my mom said, 'You have to deal with this on your own.'... I didn't want to ask my mom to help more. I knew I had got myself into this mess, so now I have to take care of it myself, but it was hard because Cayden stayed up all night, every night, for the first three weeks...My sister-in-law was a big help because she came over every day. I was surprised how much Tasha appreciated Cayden."

Bonding Takes A While

"Until the second month, I didn't want to do anything. I didn't love on Cayden until then...I did have a little of the baby blues, but I wish someone had told me everyone doesn't go through postpartum depression. Everyone had said that I was going to have it, and there was nothing I could do to stop it."

Kendra went back to school when Cayden was six weeks old. She plans on passing her high school equivalency tests and then going to college after she turns eighteen. Every morning, she and Cayden get on a bus at 7:00 a.m. and then she picks him up at the school-provided day care around 11:40 a.m.

"I felt like I couldn't take care of Cayden and go to school and still be alive. I did know it would be hard, but I didn't think it would be this hard. I was so wrong...I was also nervous about the day care he would go to while I was in school. What would they do with him?"

Things Start To Improve

Kendra's family slowly became more accepting of her role as a mother. "They saw that I was being mature and going to school and not crying and acting childish. That I'm a good mother and doing right by Cayden."

At night and when Cayden napped, Kendra would go on the internet for support from other teen moms. The site www.oneyoungparent.com was particularly helpful because she could chat with other moms there. However, she did receive a disturbing email from a twelve-year-old who was thinking about having a baby. "I told her —don't do it! You can't look for love in a baby. They don't love you until they're older." Kendra also found the book *Parenting for Dummies* helpful.

In February Cayden started sleeping better at night. Kendra also started going to church again. People didn't say anything to her about having a baby at sixteen. Her pastor would come over to the house and ask how Kendra was doing and he also offered her counseling services. Her mother's co-workers would send gifts to the house like diapers, bibs, and little toys.

Chris Drops A Bombshell

Also in February, Chris delivered an emotional blow to Kendra. "He told me that he had had sex with someone else while I was pregnant. He even laughed about it when he told me. I think because it had been so long ago. He didn't think I would be so mad. I had enough stress on me and dealing with him wasn't helping, so I broke up with him.

"We talk on the phone still, and he wants to get back together, but I just tell him how Cayden is and get off the phone. When Chris visits, I tell him to take Cayden, and I don't go along. He also told me in February that I had 'changed.' I think I wasn't back to myself yet. I had just had a baby for God's sake!

"At times I think I should get back together with him, but hopefully I never will. I really had thought we would be together forever."

Teen Mom Challenges

Kendra found that teen moms face different issues than older moms. "First off, I think dealing with the looks and opinions of people who don't even know you is hard. Then the challenges of how you are going to take care of your baby. Will the dad and his family help? What will your family think? "I wish I had talked to my mother more while I was pregnant about everything she went through. She had my sister when she was eighteen, so she could have told me more.

"I want moms to know that they don't have to stay with that dad if he's not what you want...Don't underestimate yourself. During the pregnancy, I made myself feel so bad. I could've been better. I spent all this time contacting adoption agencies and worrying about being a good mom. If I would have had the confidence I have now, I would have done better...Also, it's okay to ask for help. It doesn't mean you're not capable of taking care of your baby, it just means you're human.

"I thank God every day that I didn't give Cayden up."

AUTHOR'S REFLECTIONS

When I found out that Kendra had previously had a miscarriage, yet continued to be careless about birth control, I was confused. Why hadn't she become extra careful or thought more about how much her life would change if she had a baby? Then I remembered how often I did careless things as a teenager (please don't tell my daughters!) without thinking about the consequences. Getting "caught in the moment," as Kendra says, can lead to life-altering events. It's so hard to convey that to teenagers because they can feel immortal. I know I did at times.

What's amazing to me is how maturely Kendra handled her pregnancy and new motherhood. When you talk to her, you would think you are speaking with a woman in her twenties at least. Although it was obviously very difficult for her to become a mother at sixteen, she rose to the challenge of caring for Cayden while continuing to focus on her academic goals.

Eight months after I interviewed Kendra, I checked in with her to see how she was doing. She had passed her high school equivalency tests and was about to turn eighteen. Coincidentally, her upcoming birthday was also the day Chris was going to be released from jail. I don't know what he had been in for, but I was so relieved when she said that she was not back together with him. She was working on enrolling at college. Cayden had just turned one and was walking and talking already.

CHAPTER SIX

Jennifer M.: "I Literally Felt Like My Heart Was Being Ripped Out Of My Chest"

Jennifer had been on the Pill for six years when she and her husband, Chad, decided, in January 2004, that it was time to get pregnant. "We tried and tried, and nothing happened," Jennifer says. "In July my doctor started doing blood work, and I started getting stressed about my ability to get pregnant. I got an ovulation monitor, but I was only having a period every four months. It was not fun to have sex. I just felt discouraged."

In October 2004, Jennifer began taking Clomid, a drug that's designed to bring on ovulation. "The first round didn't even make me ovulate," she says. She still wasn't pregnant by December, so she went to a fertility specialist. "I would take the Clomid on days three through seven of my period. Then have ultrasounds starting on day eleven to determine if I was going to ovulate. Around day twenty of my cycle [in December], they found that I was going to ovulate. So they gave me a shot called Ovidrel, and I came back twenty-four hours later for the artificial insemination...The first one in December didn't work, but the one in January is what got me pregnant...I took an at-home pregnancy test on January 24th, and it was positive...We still have no idea why I had ovulation problems.

"I had a tremendous pregnancy...During the first trimester I was a little sick, but not bad at all. The hardest part of it for me was that I was a little neurotic about something going wrong. It took me so long to get pregnant, so I was always worried. That really took a toll on me." On the other hand, Jennifer was very excited to be a mother. "I never felt like I was going to be missing out on something (by becoming a mom.) I was just so thrilled and so ready."

Job And Home Choices

Jennifer knew she wanted to stay at home after the baby. "I made the decision to quit my job [as a kindergarten teacher]. I felt very lucky that I was able to do this. After my first trimester, I told my work that I would not be returning. It was a little bittersweet because I did like my job."

Since Jennifer and Chad planned to move into a house from their apartment seven weeks after the birth, they didn't set up a lot of baby equipment. "We planned for him to stay in our room for several weeks following his birth so it seemed silly to set up an entire room...It was actually kind of sad not having a baby room for him to come home to."

The couple started looking at houses when Jennifer was six months pregnant. "We closed on the house two days before birth. I would never, ever do that again or plan to move so soon after a baby."

Labor And Delivery

On September 14, 2005, around 11:30 p.m., Jennifer went to the hospital with "horrible contractions. Although my contractions were ten minutes apart, they were just so bad I couldn't take it anymore and went to the hospital even though I had been told to wait until they were five minutes apart...When they checked me, I was only two centimeters dilated and fifty percent effaced. They had me walk around the labor and delivery floor for an hour, and then I was three centimeters dilated. They called my doctor and decided to admit me at around 1:30 a.m.

"The contractions were coming every two to four minutes, and that's when I was in my worst pain. The contractions were just so above and beyond anything I had ever experienced before. About an hour later, I got my epidural, which was amazing. I did have to get two of them because they messed up on the first one—only one side of me was numb. After the second one though, I was good to go!

"They decided to break my water and start Pitocin as I wasn't progressing as fast as they wanted. After that, I progressed quickly. I started pushing at around 10:45 a.m. on September 15th. It was a pretty surreal feeling when I was pushing. I wasn't yelling or screaming like I was expecting to. I was very calm...I was just so excited. I don't think I have ever felt that kind of excitement before." Dylan was born at 11:36 a.m.

"I am sure most women would hate to hear me say this, but I had the most amazing labor and delivery ever! I loved every minute of it. Of course, I was in pain from the initial contractions, but, after the epidural, I felt like a new woman. It was just so relaxing."

Complications

At birth Dylan's crying was labored, and he struggled to get a deep breath. Jennifer says, "He was blue. They immediately suctioned from his lungs, but he still couldn't get a deep breath. They started giving him oxygen, and I knew something was wrong. I couldn't hold him, and I kept asking—'what's wrong? What's wrong?' The obstetrician said that everything was fine, but Dylan had aspirated a ton of fluid. I knew this wasn't the fairy tale delivery where they clean the baby up and bring him to you to breastfeed."

The neonatalogist, a specialist who cares for newborns, said that Jennifer could hold the baby for one picture and then they would take him down to the Neonative Intensive Care Unit (NICU.) "I was on the table getting stitched up from a tear I had during delivery, and all I knew was that something was wrong. Chad stayed with me, and they took Dylan to NICU. They didn't give Chad the option of going with the baby."

It took two hours for Jennifer to leave recovery and get settled in her hospital room. Since Dylan was in the NICU, "I was crying hysterically. I literally felt like my heart was being ripped out of my chest. As if I was having real heart pain."

Jennifer was put in a wheelchair, and she and Chad went to see Dylan in the NICU. "That was the worst moment for me. You have to scrub up, and there are, what feels like, a million babies, and they're all hooked up to things. Dylan was sleeping, but he was completely blue. He was hooked up to a million monitors. I lost it and was just hysterical. I thought—this really is serious. We went back to my room, and I cried for hours.

"Three hours later, we went back to the NICU. Dylan looked great, like a different baby...He wasn't as blue at all as he was earlier, and he had less tubes connected to him...The doctors weren't telling us much. They would say, 'He's stable, and he's on an IV, so he's getting nutrients.' They also said that his lungs looked cloudy in his chest X-ray. I was just so sad Dylan was there."

Dylan's trouble breathing led to low oxygen saturation levels in his blood. The doctors started treating him with two antibiotics because they suspected pneumonia and because his white blood count was high. Both antibiotics had to be given through an IV for seven days. "There was no room for parents to sleep in the NICU. I would come down to see Dylan all day and night, and I pumped breast-milk every three hours. The first couple of days I could just look at him, but I couldn't hold him because of all the IVs. I was scared I would rip them out."

The day after birth, Dylan's oxygen level was good, but his white blood count was up. By the third day, the 17th, he was completely out of the woods, but had to stay in the hospital to finish the seven days of antibiotics. Jennifer and Chad were finally able to hold Dylan, and Jennifer breastfed him.

Going Home Without A Baby

"I begged my doctor to diagnose me with something so I could stay at the hospital, but they released me on the 17th. I stayed at the hospital until 11:55 p.m....The nurses told me to go home and get some sleep, and I wanted to slap them. Thank goodness Dylan was better, but it was so hard to leave him in the hospital.

"When I finally left, I went outside to wait for Chad to bring the car. I started crying like I never had before. I was hyperventilating, and I was so sad that I hurt everywhere. The minute I got home, I called the hospital, and they said Dylan was fine. I was afraid that he wouldn't get watched well because he wasn't one of the sicker ones or, that if alarms went off, the nurses wouldn't rush over to him. He was at one of the best hospitals for birth in the country, but I felt no one could watch him as well as I could.

"I pretty much cried from the minute I left the hospital until I was able to get back the following morning at 7:00 a.m. Every day I was usually there from 7:00 a.m. until midnight, except for taking breaks to go out for meals. My parents rented an apartment in town for a month, and they came to the hospital a lot and we would go to dinner with them. When Chad and I did need time to ourselves though, they were great about respecting our privacy."

Jennifer's Body Shuts Down

"It was so exhausting. On the fifth day after birth, at seven at night, I hit a wall physically. I had a splitting headache and felt sick. I was so tired. I decided to go home to rest. We ordered sushi, and I lay down for a few minutes. I just couldn't relax enough to fall asleep. We went back to the hospital at 10:30, and I did feel a little better. At least my headache went away.

"I wasn't eating like I should, especially for breastfeeding. I didn't care about myself. I was pretty sore from birth, and it hurt to sit or stand. I was sore for five or six weeks from the tear and had a lot of swelling."

"I never once thought [while pregnant] that the baby would stay in the hospital. It was so shocking, the most dramatic thing ever. It probably would have stuck in the back of my mind if someone had told me that it was a possibility. It was so awful."

Jennifer bonded with some parents in the NICU. "One friend I made was constantly getting bad news about her baby, and the baby stayed in the hospital for three weeks. But then I was also surprised to see that some of the babies' parents never came in to see them.

"People would say [since the baby's in the hospital], 'Oh you can catch up on sleep and have time to relax.' I wanted to slap those people. Nobody could understand what it was like except Chad."

Dylan may have had an infection or pneumonia, but the doctors were never able to determine conclusively what was wrong.

Dylan Comes Home

Dylan was scheduled to come home on his one-week birthday. "I couldn't sleep at all the night before because I was so excited," Jennifer says. "I was also nervous that the doctor would find something wrong and not release him even though he seemed extremely healthy."

Jennifer was at the hospital early the next morning. "He was scheduled to have his last antibiotic at 1:00 p.m. and then go home at two. At 9:30 a.m., the neonatal doctor came in and said that he could go home at eleven since he had had his last antibiotic at one in the morning already. I was in heaven. Chad and my parents came, and we put Dylan in a new outfit.

"We left at eleven and videotaped the whole ride home. It was so great to leave the hospital. I had thought at times that he would never leave. It was the best day ever. I felt so lucky to have him home."

Feeding Issues

"Chad works from home and, with my parents in town, I had lots of help. I can't imagine being a single mom or not having a husband at home. Breastfeeding Dylan the first days and weeks after he was home was tricky. He wasn't a very active eater, so the feedings would take so long, and he would tend to fall asleep. I was always concerned that he wasn't getting enough...I frequently fed him pumped breast milk from a bottle. He was a difficult eater because he really never got hungry. We would wake him up during the night to eat. I think I would have enjoyed breastfeeding more if he was more of an active eater. During the feeding sessions, I would have to squeeze my breasts into his mouth and constantly wake him up because he would fall asleep after just a few swallows.

"Because Dylan was small [he weighed five and a half pounds at birth], we were told to feed him every three hours until he was nine or ten pounds...We set up alarms to feed him. All we did was feed...Luckily he gained weight quickly, but he would have projectile vomiting and throw up with every feeding. I felt like I had my shirt off all day. Breastfeeding was so much work, very hard and demanding...People had told me while I was pregnant about the difficulties of breastfeeding (one friend had even said that she hated it.) I heard all that, but thought it wouldn't be me."

When Dylan was two weeks old, a lactation consultant came to the house. "That was very helpful. She showed me different nursing holds. She also said that Dylan loved breastfeeding so much that he fell asleep while feeding because he was comfortable."

Jennifer stopped nursing after a month because of Dylan's vomiting. "I was sad to give it up, but kind of relieved. I felt sadder about it later because I felt really close to Dylan while breastfeeding. The bottle is different. I stopped cold turkey and got engorged. It was very painful. The first day I quit, we gave him formula all day. When I woke up the next morning, I breastfed Dylan. When he pulled off the breast, he threw up a lot. With the formula, he still threw up some, but not as much. Around two and a half months, that got a lot better."

New Mom Emotions

"I was surprised by how much you can love someone. I would just look at Dylan and get tears in my eyes. It was so hard to believe that my husband and I created this little being. No matter how hard he cried or how cranky he would get, I never cared. I just was so deep in love...It was hard to believe that others had gone through this because it seemed so unique. It's such an individual experience that no book can prepare you. It's all so new.

"Of course, I was fatigued beyond belief...I felt like I would never get sleep...I felt overwhelmed and stressed because I just wanted to take care of Dylan the best I possibly could. There was such a rush of so many emotions. When he would cry, I worried that he was in pain, and I couldn't figure out what was wrong. It made me nervous."

Dylan was a mellow baby, but he didn't sleep much during the day. "We didn't put him in his bed for naps, and I think that might have been a mistake," Jennifer says. "We kept him out with us.

Maybe the stimulation was too much for him. He also wanted to be held all the time.

"When difficulties did arise, the best way for me to manage them was to just take a deep breath and do the best I could. I didn't panic, and I would just keep thinking that I wasn't the first person to ever deal with these types of issues."

Marriage And Other Relationships

Jennifer had worried while pregnant about the effect a newborn would have on her marriage. "We never had a bad or strained marriage before we had a baby, but you just never know what's going to happen after the birth...I actually found it to be such a bonding experience and that it really brought us closer...It's been an extremely positive experience for our marriage."

"I was totally prepared for our schedule to revolve around the baby. That didn't surprise me. I found that my every waking thought was about Dylan. I would take Dylan everywhere with me. When he was six weeks old, we did leave him with a babysitter to attend a wedding. I didn't want to leave him, but we ended up having so much fun at the wedding. When they're so small, you're just so nervous about leaving them at first. I was so traumatized by his being in the hospital. Everything's more dangerous the first two months. I've become more comfortable as he gets bigger and is a sturdier baby."

Jennifer found it hard to make time for friendships. "I constantly felt that I had no idea what I did all day...I found that I didn't even brush my teeth until two or three in the afternoon so, of course, I wasn't able to have the same sort of relationships with my friends as I did before his birth.

"I had a few friends who had kids that were around the same age as Dylan, so it was nice for us all to get together...I found that I instantly became so close to people who were going through the same thing. Not only could they understand and answer questions regarding my baby, but they were able to understand what I was going through physically and emotionally. I sometimes found it difficult to talk to some of my friends without children."

Moving

"Since we knew we were moving soon, we were completely unorganized with Dylan's stuff. We would change his diaper on the floor and didn't really have a place for everything. Our apartment turned out to be a big mess, and we always had trouble finding things. Moving made everything a hundred times more stressful."

When it was time to move Chad "did all the packing, and we hired movers for the day of the move. All the packing and unpacking would have taken half the time without a baby. We both had an insane level of fatigue during the move. The house we moved into needs work, but what can we do with a baby here?... It's amazing how time-consuming it is to have a new baby...I would definitely never make a move so close to the birth of a child again. It was extremely difficult."

Advice For New Moms

"I think what would have helped me most was sleep, an extra pair of hands, and meals to be brought over. We often found that we would eat dinner around 10:30 at night, and it tended to be meals like Taco Bell, not a good habit to get into."

Jennifer wants new mothers not to expect to be able to read their baby's signals. "I was always told that I would just know the type of cry (whether for hunger, wet diaper, etcetera) and I found that for the first several weeks, I couldn't tell. I felt like a bad mom, like I wasn't capable of taking good care of Dylan...It just takes practice. Don't get too hard on yourself if you can't cater to your baby's every need because you can't interpret their cries.

"Every mom is going to make mistakes and it's okay. It's all about trial and error. People have been raising kids for centuries and, no matter what, your baby will be just fine."

AUTHOR'S REFLECTIONS

One of my biggest fears with both of my pregnancies was that my baby would not be able to leave the hospital with me. Jennifer's story shows how much having a child stay in the hospital strains the parents. My fears were definitely not unfounded!

If your baby does have to stay in the NICU, educate yourself as much as possible about how things work there.

Some questions you might want to ask are:

•How long will my baby be in the NICU?
•What exactly is the problem?
•What treatments and medicines will my baby have?
•May I breastfeed my baby?
•What will be their eating schedule?
•What can I do to help my baby?
•What am I allowed to bring into the NICU?
•Is it okay to hold or touch my baby?
•For how long and how often can I visit my baby?
•May I sleep in the NICU?
•How can I continue to provide care when I take my baby home?
•Is there a support group for parents with babies in the NICU?
•Is there temporary housing available (like Ronald McDonald House)?
•If so, how do we make arrangements, and do we have to pay for this housing?
•Can we eat in the NICU?
•How do we get food?

Jennifer shared a story with me about the importance of speaking up for your baby when they are ill. "A girl that I became friendly with in the NICU had a gut feeling that something just wasn't right with her baby," she says. "She felt that her baby didn't look right; that she looked really lethargic...The doctors never noticed anything, but she spoke up. The doctors finally looked into it when she kept pressuring them to, and it turned out something was seriously wrong (the baby's perfectly fine now, luckily.). Definitely speak up and let them [the doctors and nurses] know that you want to be informed of everything."

CHAPTER SEVEN

Beth N.: "I Just Wish I Had Had Somebody, Anybody, To Talk To"

Beth moved to the United States from Africa in the summer of 2000. In less than a year, she would be pregnant and facing life as a single mother.

Beth was born and raised in a small village in Kenya. After she completed school, she moved to the capital, Nairobi. To get to the United States, she applied for a green card through a lottery process. Only fifty-five thousand green cards are given out each year in Nairobi, but many more Kenyans would like to receive one. Beth was one of the lucky ones who received a green card in 2000.

Once in California, Beth found a job at a distribution warehouse. She also started coursework through an Adult Education program. In February 2001, she earned her G.E.D. (General Education Degree.)

Managing A Surprise Pregnancy

During her first autumn in the U.S., Beth became involved with a man. The following June, she learned that she was at the beginning of an unplanned pregnancy. The man she was seeing wanted her to abort the baby, but she refused, and the relationship ended soon afterwards. "I wish I had known about better forms of birth control," she says. "Also, you can't push yourself into a relationship. You should stay if you're sure there is a future, but I knew there was no future with him. We were just having a good time. That was a mistake."

The father of the baby was uninvolved during her pregnancy. Beth took childbirth preparation classes and continued to attend the local community college. "I was thinking all the time about the situation I was in," she says. "I was stressed about the break-up and hoping he would want the baby. We talked on the phone some, but not too much. I was also really missing my mom, dad, six sisters, and three brothers back home."

Beth had morning sickness for the first three to four months and not much of an appetite during that time. Once the morning sickness was over, she developed strong cravings for French fries. Her pregnancy progressed normally without any complications.

Giving Birth Alone

Beth's labor began around 8:00 p.m. on February 10, 2002. She called a friend of hers who worked at Target, but decided to wait at home until her labor pains were closer before heading to the hospital. At 4:00 a.m., she called her friend back so they could go to the hospital. When they arrived, the nurses checked Beth and found she was only dilated three centimeters. The nurses suggested that Beth come back when she was further along.

Beth returned to her house around 9:00 a.m. and her contractions started coming on stronger. "I couldn't imagine that the pains could be that bad. It surprised me when it got worse." she says. Luckily her friend was able to stay with her. By four o'clock in the afternoon, Beth felt ready to go back to the hospital.

When she got there, she was disappointed to learn she was still only at three centimeters. This time she was told that, if there was no change by the next morning, that they would send her home again. Beth's friend had to leave around 7:30 p.m., and it was very hard for Beth to deal with the labor pains alone.

"When I went to the bathroom at the hospital, there seemed to be some water coming out, but the nurses said my water hadn't broken. I asked the nurse if I could push because the pain was so bad, and it seemed like that would bring relief. She said no, but I decided to push anyway. When she came to check me soon afterwards, she said the baby was ready to come out! It only took ten minutes to push the baby out." Beth's daughter, Grace, was born at 9:11 p.m. Beth didn't take pain medication during the labor. Although she didn't have an episiotomy, a surgical cut made just before delivery to enlarge the vaginal opening, she did tear some.

Mom and baby stayed in the hospital for two days. The first day Grace wouldn't nurse. The second day she latched on better. Beth's main physical issue in the hospital was that she felt very weak.

Food, Sleep, And Depression Problems

A friend came to stay with Beth her first week home. Grace cried a lot, and Beth was afraid she didn't have enough milk for the baby. "I wasn't eating well and felt confused about the whole situation—the crying, Grace's father. I also was barely sleeping. I had never thought while pregnant about how hard it was to take care of a baby. Being woken up whenever I tried to sleep was so hard, and I had no time to cook something so I would often go without eating.

"Grace would wake up crying and I wouldn't know why. I would try to nurse and just keep trying. Rocking her helped some. I never had enough sleep, and I was so depressed. I couldn't think. Some days, I would just sit down all day. When Grace did nap, I didn't feel I could sleep because I needed to cook something for me to eat." Sometimes Beth would cook in the middle of the night, around 3:00 a.m., because that was when she felt hungry. Her eating and sleeping patterns were very erratic.

"I was so forgetful," she says. "I remember one time a friend was over, and I went into the kitchen to get her some juice. I couldn't remember how to open it! I had to get a knife to pry the top off; I didn't think to twist the top off." Beth was also suffering from headaches and struggled to make decisions. "I didn't feel like doing anything," she says. "I didn't realize that what I was feeling was depression since I had never had it before."

Beth continued to stress about her milk supply. Grace wasn't losing weight, but she wasn't gaining well. "I think if I had been eating well, I would have done better. I wish I had realized the importance of eating."

Cultural Differences

Beth also experienced difficulties because of her newness to America. "I was troubled a lot," she says, "because I didn't know about so many things. When I was pregnant, I was still figuring out how to settle down here. I wish I had found out about support groups. In Kenya, the grandparents often come for three months to stay and help. Cleaning help is hired, and the local women come over to help also. When you give birth in the village, the community comes to help out. Here, I only knew a few people through work, and my one friend who helped by taking me to the store, visiting, and shopping for me."

Beth didn't know who else to turn to for help, so she suffered for three months alone battling depression. "I thought I would be able to handle it," she says. "I knew something was wrong, but I didn't know what. I didn't feel like a bad mother, because I knew I was doing my best. I just wish I had had somebody, anybody, to talk to. Some kind of emotional support."

Beth would have liked to talk to her family back in Kenya more, but they were hard to reach. No one has a phone except for one of her brothers. "I wish I had been able to arrange for one of my parents or a relative to come help. I also wish I had cooked food beforehand and learned about the signs of depression. Maybe then I could have stopped it before it got bad.

"I was excited about having a baby, truly joyful that Grace was my daughter, but felt bad that the father wasn't concerned. Most days my head would be so heavy. It hurt to watch TV. When I sat down, I never thought of the next thing to do. Normally I'm a planner, so this was very unusual. I hardly went out those first months."

Getting Help

At three-months postpartum, Beth's doctor referred her to mental health resources. She started seeing a psychiatrist and was diagnosed with postpartum depression. She also started taking Prozac.

The psychiatrist advised her to go out with the baby more—to get out and talk to people. "Getting out really helped," she says. "I started going to International House [a place where people from different countries can get together.] They have a weekly meeting where you can talk and get to know each other...I would feel good when I went out or met people."

Unfortunately, possibly from being isolated so much, Grace would cry often when they were out. Although the crying was stressful, Beth continued to try new things. One time when they went to visit the family that had first hosted Beth when she came to the U.S., Grace cried for four hours. No one could figure out what was wrong. "I wasn't embarrassed that she was crying, but I was embarrassed because everyone was talking about it. There was nothing I could do. I guess she was afraid of new people."

Beth began taking Grace to a playgroup at a family resource center and that helped, along with continuing to expose her to new activities. She eventually became a very social baby.

Beth's depression improved with the Prozac and therapy, but she was still too ill to work. Luckily, she was able to obtain disability benefits because of the depression. When Grace was six months old, Beth started back at college by taking one class. "I did feel better when I started back at school. I was meeting people and gaining confidence. Since I was feeling better, I stopped the Prozac for a while, but I became depressed again and went back on medication. I had been afraid that the medication would have negative breastfeeding effects, but realized that it was too important for me to be well." Beth stayed on Prozac until Grace was about a year old and then successfully weaned herself from the medication.

Advice For Other Moms

Beth feels it's important for new mothers to have friends around to support you and to join a support group. These contacts can introduce you to organizations or groups where you can get more help. "Try and talk about depression so that more people are aware," she says. She also thinks she wouldn't have suffered postpartum depression if she had been at home in Kenya. "I've never heard of someone having postpartum depression back home. In Kenya, you knew what your neighbors were doing. When someone has a baby, in two hours everybody in the village knows. You've all known each other's families from way back. Here people are too busy. There are so many people from different beliefs and different parts of the world. People are very cautious of their neighbors. It's so hard to get close to people.

"I didn't have much chance to talk to new mothers [during postpartum] and that would've helped. I also wish I had had time to look for a church to go to. Everybody goes through postpartum in a different way. I wish I had known more about what to expect."

AUTHOR'S REFLECTIONS

Americans could learn a lot from other countries about how to nurture new families. In Asian cultures, the time after birth is called the "month" (although it can be longer than a month), and the new mother is brought nourishing foods and soups and allowed to stay in bed as much as she needs. In Africa and South America, the new mother is treated like a queen for six weeks or longer— everything is done for her.

Anthropologist Dana Raphael studied postpartum traditions in over two hundred cultures and found the common denominators were large amounts of time and energy given to the brand new mother. Even animals seem to get this better than Americans. For example, we usually think of a male gorilla as having a harem of females around him. In reality, those females are a sort-of sisterhood. When one of them gives birth, all the other females take care of her.

For many women in America, like Beth, once they give birth, they are left alone after only a few days. The need for physical and emotional support for these women is huge. On top of the isolation many new mothers here feel, Beth had the added burden of adjusting to a new culture. After I interviewed Beth, I felt so sorry that this was her introduction to how new mothers are treated, and often abandoned, in the U.S. I wished that she could have enjoyed nurturing like she would have received back in her Kenyan village.

Knowing the warning signs of postpartum depression can also help new mothers be aware of when it's time to seek help and reduce their suffering sooner. From the Postpartum Support International website, www.postpartum.net, the following information can help you determine whether you are experiencing baby blues or postpartum depression:

Baby Blues:

• Occurs in about eighty percent of mothers
• Usual onset within first week postpartum
• Symptoms may persist up to three weeks

Symptoms:

• Mood instability
• Weepiness
• Sadness
• Anxiety
• Lack of concentration
• Feelings of dependency

Postpartum Depression and/or Anxiety

• Occurs in fifteen to twenty percent of mothers
• Onset is usually gradual, but it can be rapid and begin any time in the first year

Symptoms:

• Excessive worry or anxiety
• Irritability or short temper
• Feeling overwhelmed, difficulty making decisions

- Sad mood, feelings of guilt, phobias
- Hopelessness
- Sleep problems (often the woman cannot sleep or sleeps too much), fatigue
- Physical symptoms or complaints without apparent physical cause
- Discomfort around the baby or a lack of feeling toward the baby
- Loss of focus and concentration (may miss appointments, for example)
- Loss of interest or pleasure, decreased libido
- Changes in appetite; significant weight loss or gain

Risk factors:

- Fifty to eighty percent risk if previous postpartum depression
- Depression or anxiety during pregnancy
- Personal or family history of depression/anxiety
- Abrupt weaning from breastfeeding
- Social isolation or poor support
- History of premenstrual syndrome (PMS) or premenstrual dysphoric disorder (PMDD)
- Mood changes while taking birth control pill or fertility medication, such as Clomid
- Thyroid dysfunction

For more resources on postpartum depression, see Appendix A.

CHAPTER EIGHT

Eleanor: "The Hardest Thing Was How Hormonal I Felt"

"It's like losing a month of your life," is how Eleanor(names have been changed) describes giving birth four weeks early. Although she didn't love being pregnant, she would have much rather carried her baby to full-term. "I didn't feel prepared because I thought I had another month to get ready," she says.

Eleanor's due date was June 28th, but she woke up at 3:00 a.m. on Memorial Day 2003 because her water had broken. She went to the hospital and found that her baby was fine on the fetal heart monitor. The staff told her that she could go for a few days after the water broke, so she was free to go home, or they could induce labor.

She chose to leave the hospital and spent the day shopping for baby items with her husband, Michael. "I was nervous about the traffic coming back from shopping since I was having mild contractions, but we got back home fine and had dinner and went for a long walk," she says. She and Michael also took some pictures of themselves in the backyard. "It was sad to think it was our last day as just the two of us. We'd been married nine years and together twelve, so this was going to be a big change."

The Birth

Around 3:30 a.m. the next morning, Eleanor woke with more contractions and went into the hospital at 9:00 a.m. When they checked her cervix, she was told that she was dilated between two and three centimeters. "That was hard. It was discouraging because I wasn't further along." As hours passed, Eleanor's labor was not progressing, so the medical team decided to use Pitocin to induce labor. "The contractions became more intense and closer together even though they were upping it [the Pitocin] slowly." Eventually the doctor increased the Pitocin at a faster rate. "I was nervous about having an epidural, but now I wish I had done it. I did ask for pain relief, and they gave me a narcotic drip, but it didn't help much." Ten minutes after getting the drip, Eleanor felt the need to push. "I felt horrible, horrific pain, and the pushing took between forty-five minutes to an hour. Since I had had to fend off earlier impulses to push, it was difficult to access that energy later. At least once I reached the pushing stage, however, I knew there would be an end."

It had been a long day in the hospital when Eleanor's daughter, Katie, was born at 10:51 p.m. During delivery, Eleanor's hands, face, and chest went numb, and she was administered an oxygen mask. "The oxygen mask helped. I think I was hyperventilating which caused the numbness."

Even though Katie was a month early, her health was good, and she weighed five pounds, fifteen ounces. She cried right away and showed no signs of distress.

Hormonal And Breastfeeding Issues

Katie developed a slight case of jaundice, so Eleanor and the baby stayed at the hospital for five days. At two-days postpartum, Eleanor was thrilled when her mom arrived from out of town, but also found herself weepy and on edge. "Michael tried to videotape us—the three generations of women—but I kept crying. By far the hardest thing was how hormonal I felt. I was blindsided by it. I felt unable to cope, like I was a total wreck. I thought I'd be okay, but at moments couldn't handle things. My hormonal changes were very confusing for Michael since I had never been like this before."

Eleanor was also stressed about how much Katie was eating since the baby was premature. "Katie would latch on to my breast for a few seconds, then let go. Sometimes it would take an hour to get her latched on. Nursing felt like an eternity those first weeks, plus I was worried that, if she didn't eat, the jaundice would get worse. My worries were irrational and unpredictable.

"Luckily, Katie was a good sleeper and would sleep for two to three hours stretches. One nurse told me to wake her up to nurse, but I would try, and she would just fall back asleep at the breast. I did find that standing up and nursing while bouncing the baby worked a little. One nurse said, 'You don't want to do what with a premie. She'll just fall asleep.' I knew she was wrong and that what I was doing worked. Eventually I just did what I felt was best...Since nursing took forever, I remember thinking—am I going to be doing this for a long time? I would get nervous when I knew it was time to nurse and worry about if Katie would latch on well or not. Plus I thought, 'Oh my God, I will struggle with this again in three hours, and I'm so tired.'"

First Days And Nights At Home

Eleanor has strong memories of her first night home from the hospital. "Starting around 11 p.m., I breastfed Katie or used a syringe to feed her until 12:30 a.m. She was nursing so fussily that I was afraid she wasn't getting enough, and my milk would dry up. I was truly terrified that I was starving the baby. Katie would latch on for five sucks and then latch off and look around. I couldn't get the breast pump to work. I was panicked. I thought I had nothing to feed her. I woke Michael up and asked him to go to the hospital for extra parts for the pump.

"He brought the parts back, and I was able to pump. I still couldn't get Katie to latch on for long, so I thought I would have to give her something in a bottle. Later that morning, around 4:00 a.m., I got her to latch on for twelve solid minutes. I was so relieved. I felt like she finally got it.

"I remember one friend telling me during those early days— just think, all around the world right now, there are women breastfeeding. That gave me some perspective and helped me to not feel so alone."

Eleanor contacted a lactation consultant, Christy, to address her breastfeeding problems. Christy came to the house the first week and returned again around one month postpartum. Eleanor also phoned Christy close to a dozen times to get answers to her breastfeeding questions. "It helped so much to know Christy was there," she says.

Appetite And Sleep Problems

Along with the breastfeeding challenges, Eleanor noticed that she could get obsessive with worry, particularly in the late afternoons. "It's not that anything would be so wrong, but I just couldn't talk about anything rationally." The anxiety led to intestinal problems and caused Eleanor's appetite to drop. Her doctor suggested that she try an anti-depressant. "Even though I never took it, I was relieved to have a back-up," she says. She also started following the bland BRAT diet (Bananas, Rice, Applesauce, Toast) to help with her stomach discomfort. The diet helped along with drinking a half glass of wine in the evening to relax.

"I had a lot of sleep issues," Eleanor adds. "I was anxious when it was time to sleep if I couldn't. Sometimes, I would take a quarter dose of Tylenol PM to help me sleep which was okayed by my doctor."

Eleanor read somewhere to ask herself the following questions when she was anxious about the baby: 1) Is the baby gaining weight?, 2) Is the pediatrician okay with the baby's development?, and 3) Is the baby most of the time coping or doing okay?

If she could answer, Yes, to all three questions, Eleanor felt assured that she was doing all right.

"What amazes me is no one told me what it could be like. I had all of these positives—my husband was home to help, Katie is a good sleeper, I knew I didn't have to go back to work for six months, and Katie did eventually become a good nurser. Still, it was very hard. I knew in a vague way it would be hard, but didn't know how hard. I felt overwhelmed, stressed, and isolated. Also, no one ever said that baby blues could last longer than three to five days. Mine was better at three weeks, and much better at six weeks. I think we need a different name for it. Baby blues diminishes how tough it can be.

"Even if everything is fine with your baby, you can still expect to be really emotional and freaked out. I felt hyperemotional, as if I could cry at any time. I wish someone had said to me while I was pregnant that they had been an emotional basket case after they had their baby. My friends hadn't told me, but then, when I brought it up later, they all said they had felt the same thing."

"Shouldness" During The Childbearing Year

"I think women are made to feel diminished and wrong throughout pregnancy and postpartum. People should bite their tongues. One woman said to me, 'You must be so enjoying this time and be so in love with your baby.' I burst into tears because I didn't feel that way at all at the time...You're so vulnerable that fairly normal or innocuous remarks can really set you off. It seems to me that there's a huge amount of 'shouldness' surrounding pregnancy, childbirth, and child rearing. I recently formulated the notion that the word 'should' ought to be completely omitted from all conversations with new parents. It's so unhelpful.

"Two books that I feel are quite good about not conveying a sense of 'shouldness' are, *Dr. Spock's Baby and Child Care*, and a book by the American Pediatric Association called, *Caring for your Baby and Young Child (Birth to Age 5.)* I didn't like the book, *What to Expect When You're Expecting*. I call the authors Food Nazis. Whenever you take a bite of food when you're pregnant, they advise you to ask yourself, 'Is this the best bite for my baby?' They make it sound like all you are is a baby carrier...In general I found that most books provided lots of practical advice (like how to change a diaper), but didn't include information on how to cope with the huge psychological, organizational, and financial changes a baby causes in your life."

Changing Relationships

"Since Katie's birth, I have a deeper connection with my friends with kids. The bond intensifies. But with one friend who

71

doesn't have kids, and isn't planning on it, things became difficult. I felt like I was imposing on her when I talked about Katie so, although I understand, I limit how much I talk to her about the baby.

"Michael and I also had a couple of great, big fights those first months postpartum. He felt neglected. During one fight, he said, 'I've lost you to the baby. I never get any part of you.' It's important to not get completely absorbed with the baby. I tried to be aware of that, but it's not always easy. My being so emotional was hard for Michael. He was mad because he didn't know how to handle it. I was the one who pushed to have a baby, and Michael always knew it would be hard. So when I wasn't coping, Michael felt like—well, you got me into this. He wanted things to be the way they were. For example, during the first week home, Michael wanted to invite friends over for coffee. That was just too huge for me. He always tells me I'm doing a great job, but he doesn't get why I was so surprised with how hard it is."

Eleanor's family came to help at two different times during the first months. When they left after the second visit, she and Michael fought about Eleanor's emotional state. "Michael just didn't get how hard it was for me when my family left. Most men don't get this. At times, I was also upset with Michael's lack of interest in the baby. He will let her cry longer than I would before he does something. It hits my nerve. During the fight, I even suggested that Katie and I should go away for a while so Michael didn't have to cope with us. He was really mad about that and said, 'You're not taking my baby away.'"

Helpful Comments From Others

"What would have been helpful would be for people to say, 'Take it one day at a time. Do what's best for you and your baby. Don't worry so much. You may get obsessive and worry about things, especially at certain times of the day.' My mom was great about this, very supportive. The message I got from her was that I was doing great. She said, 'I know it's hard. It was hard for me too.' She wasn't judgmental and didn't question how I did things. She was also good about anticipating my needs and being sensitive to both mine and Michael's needs. I remember I craved apple juice, and my mom stocked the fridge with it. A piece of advice she gave me also was, 'Don't expect to get anything done the first three months. Then, anything you do get done, you can feel good about yourself.'"

One of Eleanor's friends said that she hoped Eleanor felt a great sense of achievement to have Katie thriving so well. She also told Eleanor that people don't tell new parents enough about what a good job they're doing. Eleanor says, "It was so helpful and encouraging. I'm going to have to make a mental note to do the same, because even when you've been through to the other side, I think it can be hard to remember. You just have to let go of control for a while—both emotional and mental control."

How To Help Yourself

Slowly Eleanor found things that made her feel better. "Just getting out helped. Sometimes it can feel like too much, but it's worth the effort. Going into work to show off the baby, getting a haircut, or a massage. Talking to other mothers was the most helpful. The joyful moments though were less than expected and that was confusing.

"I wish I had made a list in advance of people that could help me: a lactation consultant, postpartum doula, housecleaner, friends. If you're not surrounded by family and friends, you should get a doula. Make it a huge priority to be close to your own mother or your mother-in-law if possible. Either move closer to family or have the option of going there.

"Every day have somebody that you are going to call or have someone come over to check on you. I had a colleague, a mother of a six-month old, who wrote and told me how hard it was. She said for her it got better between day seventy and day one hundred. I had to laugh that she had been counting the days. It just reinforced that you're not automatically better at six weeks.

"The internet was more helpful to me than books. I would search under 'breastfeeding problems' and read about what other people had gone through and what worked."

More Ideas

While in the hospital, Eleanor advises moms to "take advantage of the help. It's better to be assertive and ask questions while you're there. Once you're home, don't hesitate to call the advice nurse even if it's three in the morning.

"What helped me too was to get myself back into work early and gradually. My work isn't anxiety-provoking, which is a big plus. If not work, then a hobby or something just for you. Do something before you've completely lost your identity."

Eleanor also wishes she had prepared the house more. "Setting up a breastfeeding area in advance with a Boppy pillow and other supplies would have been good. Also, since I was so worried about Katie getting enough to eat, I wish I had had a couple of bottles of formula on hand. I didn't need it, but I wouldn't have panicked so much. In every area, have supplies already there."

Although at times Eleanor has felt like parenthood can just "be too much," she feels it's all been worth the effort. She also wants to make it better for other new parents. She feels that there's often a ridiculous attitude in our culture of "if you do everything perfectly (as a new parent), you could prevent anything bad from happening." She adds, "I've been lucky to meet almost none of this attitude in person, but even when people are being very neutral and mild, I'm sensitive to the lightest criticism of my parenting...New parents, especially new mothers, are extremely vulnerable to this kind of thing."

AUTHOR'S REFLECTIONS

If your baby arrives early, like Eleanor's, it's not too late to do something to avoid the isolation of being home with a newborn. Be aware that you are more at risk for depression if you don't have regular adult contact.

In her book, *At-Home Motherhood: Making It Work For You*, author Cindy Tolliver refers to the isolation as the "Home Alone Syndrome" and provides ideas for avoiding it. Seek out neighbors who stay home, play groups, and parent groups. Attend one of the parent/child classes offered by recreation departments, hospitals, and churches. You could even start your own parenting group and/or babysitting cooperative by putting up a flyer or placing an ad to find other parents who want to share experiences and provide each other with valuable tips. Visiting with co-workers, like Eleanor did, also can help.

Although you may feel you don't have a second to spare, don't neglect your own interests. Mothers can easily fall into the trap of looking after everyone else's needs and ignoring their own. Exercising (once you have your doctor's okay), playing a musical instrument, and even reading novels can help.

Change your expectations. Most new mothers are amazed at how little they get done during the day—and they don't even take a coffee break or a lunch hour! This may be tough if you are used to being a super-productive person on the job. Realize that parenting is life at a different pace and that being a relaxed, happy parent is more important than a fully checked-off "to do" list.

Remember too what Eleanor mentioned—there seems to be a lot of "shoulds" about parenting. Trust your instincts, but don't be afraid to seek advice from supportive people you respect. Every family is different, and there are no universal rules for raising children. You will find the mothering path that works best for you, but it takes time. Don't be hard on yourself when you feel uncertain about what to do. Every mother (if they're honest!) will tell you that they've felt the same way at times.

CHAPTER NINE

Melissa: "I Felt Like I Was A Failure [For Having A C-Section]"

"**M**y husband, Steven, called my pregnancy the most planned thing of his life," Melissa says. "We had been married six months and were very excited...I got pregnant on the first try...This would be the first grandchild, and I was the first one in my group of friends to get pregnant."

Melissa loved being pregnant. "I was very active during the pregnancy. The baby growing inside me was like watching a science experiment."

Concern About The Baby's Size

At eight months, Melissa's doctor became worried that the baby's stomach measurement was small. "I had an ultrasound, and they were also worried that the baby's trunk was smaller than it should be. I started having non-stress tests twice a week which actually caused me a lot of stress!"

When Melissa went to her doctor's office on July 20th, "My doctor said, 'Something's wrong (with the baby.)' The doctors in the practice wanted to do a cesarean section even though my due date wasn't until September 7th. Then they called in a specialist who said it was okay to keep monitoring and to not have a c-section right away."

Melissa's baby was breech, so on Friday, August 13th, her doctor tried to turn the baby by using his hands on her abdomen (a procedure called "external cephalic version" or "ECV.") It didn't work for Melissa's baby. "I'm not a religious person, but I prayed a lot during that time that the baby would be okay. I cried a lot and wrote in my journal. I also tried acupuncture to get the baby turned, but that didn't work either."

Around the same time, Melissa's doctor said the baby looked like he was getting bigger. "I knew I might have to have a c-section because he was breech, but I thought I would at least get to my due date."

At 11 a.m. the following Tuesday, Melissa went to a different doctor in her practice to try ECV again. "I was so confident that this doctor would turn the baby that day. I had heard she had success turning another baby, and she was also an osteopath [a holistic doctor], so I felt she was more 'tuned' into the procedure."

Unplanned Delivery

When the doctor tried to turn the baby, the baby's heart rate dropped. "The doctor said, 'Let's take him out.' I was not ready for that at all. I had told my office at work, 'I'll be back in two hours,' when I left for the doctor's appointment. The baby's room at home was not put together because I was planning on doing a lot of baby prep after my last day of work which was suppose to be the next day. I was striving for a natural childbirth and had hired a birth doula. I wasn't physically or emotionally ready to have the baby then. I wanted to know what labor would be like and felt the moment was taken from me."

Melissa was sent to the hospital and at 4:00 p.m. was told by her doctor that it was time to "take the baby out." "I felt terrible," Melissa says. "I started crying and was very worried about the baby because he didn't move for the ultrasound. I also felt selfish because I didn't want the c-section. I was shocked that the baby was coming tonight. I had only had one thing to eat all day because of the turning, and I wondered if that didn't contribute to his lack of activity. I asked later and was told, no, that that wouldn't cause a problem."

Nicole, Melissa's birth doula, arrived between 5:00 and 6:00 p.m. "She [Nicole] was the one person I asked at the hospital if we were doing the right thing. I turned to her for an alternative view, and she told me that, yes, we were doing the right thing."

Before her c-section, Melissa's doctor told her and Steven, "If there's a chance there's something wrong with the baby, we'll have to airlift him to another hospital, and you won't be able to see him." "That scared the hell out of us," Melissa says. Melissa's son, Kaiden, was born at 8:32 p.m. on August 17, 2004 and had no health problems. He weighed six pounds, three ounces. "After the c-section [while still in the operating room], I was really shaky. I felt so groggy. They brought the baby over, but I couldn't move my arms to hold him. I also couldn't cry, and I thought I should be."

Depression Hits

Melissa feels that her three days in the hospital were good, but things changed when she started packing up to go home. "This overwhelming sadness came over me. I wanted to cry, but didn't know why. I sat down and bawled. When I got home, it hit me: Oh my God, I didn't give birth. I felt I had missed a sacred passage that every woman is entitled to have. I might never have a natural childbirth. That's when I really fell into a depression.

"I didn't want to take care of Kaiden. I felt like I didn't deserve him because I just laid on a table for birth. I felt like I was a failure and that I got cheated. I was sad and angry."

Once home, Melissa started playing What If? games in her mind. "What if I hadn't come back in to have him turned? What if I had spoken up more with the doctors? What if I had asked to wait one day?...I was angry at the doctors, my doula, and myself for not speaking up more." Melissa's depression was the worst at night when she would end up laying in bed sobbing.

Melissa adds, "I knew that when Kaiden was a year old that we would try to get pregnant again. At times I thought I wouldn't get to the next August...Also certain triggers made things worse like seeing a pregnant woman or seeing close friends who were pregnant."

Frustration With Others

"My doula came to see me about a week after Kaiden's birth and I told her how I was feeling about the c-section. She told me then that she and Linda, my birthing class teacher, had talked before Kaiden was born. They thought that the doctors were being overly cautious, and a c-section wasn't necessary. She said she just didn't want to put me in a bad position with my doctors, but isn't that her job as a doula, to act as a go-between between patient and doctor?"

Steven didn't understand what Melissa was going through. He would say, "We have a healthy baby. We need you. The baby needs you." Along with the stress of the depression, Steven only could take a week off from work after Kaiden was born. Melissa's mom and sister came to help for the first two weeks.

"People would say they were sorry about me having the c-section and that would kill me. Other comments like: 'Oh, but you have a healthy baby,' or, 'You're so lucky that you didn't have to go through labor,' were also painful. It would have been better if people just would have listened and encouraged me for the next time. People were surprised that I was so upset about the c-section."

Despite the depression, Melissa says, "Being a parent is also like falling in love. Every day, you love him [the baby] more because you're getting to know him more. We made this person, and it's amazing."

Breastfeeding Problems

Nursing had gone well in the hospital with only a "little bit of a problem" with Kaiden latching on, but breastfeeding difficulties arose at home. Melissa's nipples became sore and cracked with some bleeding. "The baby would cry, and I'd be like, 'No!' He would latch on okay, but my nipples needed to get broken in. Also, letdown [the milk ejection reflex] was painful." Letdown occurs just before nursing and may be accompanied by a tingling sensation, milk leaking out of the breast, or pain as in Melissa's case.

Two weeks after birth, Melissa was driving her sister to the airport and started not feeling well. "I had a fever of one hundred and one and it felt like my right breast had a huge knot in it. I felt like I had the flu. Steven was back at work, and everyone was gone. I had so much more respect for what my mother went through!" It turns out Melissa had developed mastitis, an inflammation of the breast that may include infection. She took Motrin, used a heating pad on her breast, and massaged it out. Twenty-four hours later, she was much better. Letdown continued to be painful though, particularly on her left breast. That lasted for about a month and a half, and then everything about breastfeeding "got better."

"What surprised me about breastfeeding was how much time you spend doing it. I became hooked on TV because all you did was sit there. I think it's good advice to only find one goal a day for yourself when you're nursing...Also, as soon as you can in the morning, just brush your teeth, splash your face with water, and change into something comfy...It will make you feel more a part of the world and not so grubby."

What Helped Those Early Weeks

Melissa had a lot of visitors the first weeks including friends who brought meals twice a week for a month. "I liked getting visitors. It made me feel more in touch with everyone and not so isolated. Plus I liked showing off Kaiden. Sometimes it even gave me a reason to get dressed!"

Luckily, sleep wasn't a big problem with Kaiden. "He'd get up twice in the night, around two or three and then again at six, after going to bed at 10:00 p.m...He slept in bed with us, and it was the most natural thing in the world. It was easier on me. I would barely wake up enough to put my breast in his mouth and then would go back to sleep."

What also helped Melissa was taking a deep breath when she felt overwhelmed. "Getting out of the house did help," she says. "It might take an hour to leave the house, but it was worth it. Then I would feel part of the world. Kaiden would calm down on walks.

Being social with other moms also helped. Also, parking in one place and walking to do a bunch of errands so I didn't have to deal with the car seat."

"Focusing on the baby" was key for Melissa. "I would think, yeah, birth sucked, but look what I have. He needs me."

Identity Issues

"After my mom left, I thought, who's the adult now? Who am I to be raising a child? The hardest part was the time not being my own...You barely have time to go to the bathroom or feed yourself. Since Kaiden always wanted to be held, I would put him in the sling often. Sometimes that would keep me from changing out of my pajamas until two in the afternoon.

"When Kaiden was five weeks old, I took him on his first walk in a stroller. It was like an out-of-body experience where I could see myself and wondered, who are you? I'd been an independent woman and now, I thought, 'I am such a housewife.'

Melissa found claims about getting your body back when you are breastfeeding inaccurate. When I interviewed her, at ten-months postpartum, she hadn't lost all her baby weight despite being an active person during pregnancy and as much as she could postpartum. "They say you're burning all these calories when you breastfeed, but your body is storing fat. You don't wear some of your clothes for two years. I like to exercise, but had to go really slowly because of the c-section. It's major abdominal surgery. You don't bounce back. Also, I hated the scar and felt mutilated whenever I looked at it.

"The isolation was hard. One time I was so frustrated. I needed to get out. I went to the post office and got stuck in traffic. I started crying. I just couldn't get anything done because Kaiden wouldn't be put down. That did get better around three months."

What She Wishes Had Been Different

"I wish I had had more people to talk to about the c-section. I wish the doctor had been more sensitive to the emotional impact of c-sections...They don't want to think about your emotional health. I don't fault the doctor personally, but I don't even want to deal with the medical establishment with the next baby. I'm going to do a home birth. I would never succumb to another c-section.

"I wish I had started reading about babies earlier...No one tells you how many decisions you have to make like circumcision, vaccines, and other issues...I think pregnant women should do a lot of reading. Trust your instincts. Don't trust the doctors implicitly. Question them. Don't let them pressure you...Empower yourself. Also, cut yourself a break. The first two to three months you're not going to be where you were before the baby. Devote your time to the baby."

"What I think would have helped me the most, but is not available in the small town where I live, is a c-section support group. It would be helpful to talk to other women who have gone through the same thing."

At six-weeks postpartum Melissa's mom came back to help out for two weeks and then her mother-in-law came for a week after that. "I tell moms to hang on for two to three months and then things get better. The baby finally smiles. You finally get a reward. It's a joy to watch them discover things."

Work And Emotional Struggles

When Kaiden was three months old, Melissa returned to work. Her plan was to work three days a week for eight hours a day. "My marriage didn't get strained until I returned to work. Steven didn't think I should go back. He wanted me to take another month...He would watch Kaiden on Mondays, Tuesdays, and Wednesdays, and I would watch him the rest of the time. Although that plan looked good on paper, it didn't work in reality. Men just don't have it in them—the maternal instinct...Steven thought he could stay home with the baby, but one day a week was it.

"In January, we hired a babysitter, and then I ended up leaving my job in April. Now I teach and do freelance work. What would probably work best is for me to work one to two days a week with a couple of half days."

Melissa's depression over the c-section continued. "I did eventually go to counseling when Kaiden was seven months old. I didn't think I had the time, but my mom said, 'You have to make the time.'" The counselor specializes in bereavement. "I do find it helpful, but I am not totally there yet...Therapy has helped me just to be able to talk to someone every time a 'trigger' comes up. Like when one of my friends has a baby, it's always very hard for me. It brings up a lot of emotions."

Lessons Learned

"I learned [in therapy] that I have issues with challenging authority and potentially getting involved in a conflict. I don't want to 'rock the boat.' So, instead of disagreeing with someone, I demure in order to prevent an uncomfortable situation...On one hand, I know that I did the best I could given the circumstances, but I also know that next time will be different, and I will speak up if the situation calls for it. My experience has also helped me to be a better advocate for my son and to stand up to his doctor when I don't believe she is right."

"The thing that has made me feel the most at peace with the delivery is the thought that it happened for a reason. I don't believe it was a medical one, but more the belief that the total disappointment and frustration and sadness of this experience will make my next child's birth that much more special...I would trade twenty-four to forty-eight hours of labor pain for the seven months of anguish I felt...I know I will do everything in my power to avoid another c-section."

AUTHOR'S REFLECTIONS

The cesarean section rate in the United States is over 29% and has increased more than forty percent since 1996 according to the National Center for Health Statistics. Many doctors, midwives, and obstetrical nurses feel the rate is much higher than is necessary. Speculation about our high c-section rates include: fear of malpractice lawsuits by the doctors, scheduling c-sections for the doctor's or the mother's convenience, and the desire of women to avoid the pain of labor by planning a c-section.

Of course, there are many medical reasons that merit a c-section. However, just like in a vaginal delivery, the new mother is often not prepared for what to expect afterwards, emotionally and physically. Don't wait until your due date to find out what conditions your doctor or midwife believe necessitate a c-section. Think through your feelings on the choices and outcomes before you have to deal with it in what could be a very stressful situation. If you are hiring a birth doula, be sure they know where you stand on these issues also.

From my work as a postpartum doula, I've observed firsthand how a c-section recovery can be more difficult and longer than a vaginal birth recovery. Keep that in mind if you have the option of having a planned c-section or could try for a vaginal delivery.

If you do have a c-section, the following suggestions from parenthoodweb.com can help ease your recovery:

• Get out of bed and move around, but be careful not to overdo it.
• Avoid lifting anything heavier than your baby.
• You will be directed not to drive for a specific amount of time (usually two to three weeks, but it can be longer); adhere to these recommendations.
• Get help with your baby, other children, and housework. If necessary, let the housework slide.
• Ask your care provider when you can exercise. Then join a postpartum exercise class designed for women recovering from c-sections (these are usually available through your local hospital).
• Expect that it may take several months, or longer, before you feel like yourself again.

Don't be surprised if you find yourself grieving your birth experience. While pregnant, it can be hard to imagine that you will end up needing a c-section. If you do have one, you are not a failure, just one of millions of mothers in the same situation.

CHAPTER TEN

Samantha: "I Was Surprised By The Shear 'Nonstopness' Of Parenthood"

After talking about having a child for over six months, Samantha and her partner, Heather, decided to seek the services of a sperm bank. They chose a donor I.D. program, which would give their child the option at age eighteen of contacting the sperm donor if they wish.

"We would get a list of donors to review from the bank," Samantha says. "Each profile lists the donor's medical background, physical traits, occupation, income, ethnicity, education, hobbies, etcetera. The profile also lists the reason why they are donating. We wanted someone with a similar ethnic background to Heather [since Samantha would be carrying the baby], so possibly the baby would look like us! We didn't want alcoholism in the donor's background because I have that in my family."

Samantha took her temperature every morning to determine when she was ovulating. "We would pick three to five different donors from the sperm bank list, test if I was ovulating, and then call the sperm bank...If they didn't have any sperm of the first person on our list, they would go to the next. It's an ongoing donation system for the donors, so they store what they have and then, as they come in with more, they store that, too. They will keep some for people to have siblings with the same donor. We already bought some to have a sibling in the future. They are storing it for us—at a fee, of course."

Since her health insurance didn't cover insemination, Samantha and Heather did the procedure themselves the first three months. "We lived in Oregon at the time, and the sperm bank was in California. They would Federal Express the sperm on dry ice. You insert the sperm with a syringe, elevate your pelvis, and then lay down for an hour. They would send two vials each month since they say to do the insemination two days in a row. Each vial was $250, and it cost $100 each time to ship them.

"The fourth month we moved to California so we went to the sperm bank, and they did the insemination there. That cost $1,000, which included the cost of the vials." The fourth insemination took, which was lucky because the couple had been told it typically takes six months to a year to get pregnant.

Preparing For The Baby

Samantha's pregnancy went pretty smoothly. "I had a little morning sickness. Otherwise, being tired was the biggest physical symptom (other than getting big.) Emotionally I had a hard time because I felt not in control of my body. I would be feeling fine and then, all of a sudden, I would be starving and grumpy. I didn't like feeling tired all the time. I'm a person who is busy and likes to do, do, do. I was excited about becoming a mom, but it felt a little unreal even then.

"We bought baby stuff and got lots of gifts. I also talked to other people with small children and asked them what we really needed for the baby...We had a friend who had done a lot of research and told us of brands that tended to have a lot of recalls and brands that didn't have very many."

Samantha and Heather took a birthing class and a breastfeeding class. The teacher in the birthing class did tell them, "It's important for the partner to take care of the mom," but nothing else was said about how to address a new mom's emotional needs. "We hired my cousin [Anna, a college student] to come stay with us for eight weeks after the baby was born because Heather was going to be finishing her dissertation."

Birth Day

Samantha started experiencing contractions about a week before her due date. The contractions would get closer together, but not stronger. "My whole stomach would feel tight during contractions, sometimes for fifteen minutes," she says.

On Wednesday, Samantha went into the doctor's office and was told she was dilated two centimeters. To get labor moving along, the doctor stripped her membranes, a procedure where the practitioner places her gloved finger through the cervix and sweeps the amniotic membranes free of their attachment to the lower part of the uterine cavity. On Thursday and Friday, the contractions came closer together. Samantha's doctor told her, "If you can still talk (during a contraction), they're not strong enough.

"I knew our doctor would be on call on Sunday," Samantha says, "so I called her that morning and she said, 'I can't believe you haven't had that baby yet.' We went to the hospital after a quick lunch. The doctor broke my water around 3:00 p.m.

"Breathing through contractions saved me. There were very few that I thought—I can't do this. Heather and my mom were there, and I was on an IV for fluids, but I could walk around."

Around 9:00 p.m., Samantha was ready to push. "It was a crazy night (at the hospital), and my doctor ended up delivering seven babies that night. The woman next door wanted to push right after I started pushing, so the nurses kept coming back and forth to give the doctor updates. The doctor said the other woman could wait because she had had an epidural and wasn't feeling anything, and I was feeling everything.

"I was so focused on pushing, but when the doctor asked me not to push during a contraction I was like, wow, I am still feeling contractions...After pushing for almost an hour, I started to use the squat bar and that made a huge difference. That was when I felt like we were making progress." Zachary was born at 11:02 p.m. on Sunday, June 20, 2004.

Sleep Problems In The Hospital

"The whole night Sunday, I was too keyed up to sleep," Samantha says. "I was exhausted after delivery, but I just kept looking at Zach and thinking—he's really here...Then Monday morning, I was given a roommate who was around nineteen. She had tons of people come by to visit. We told her we needed to sleep, and she didn't seem to understand." Visiting hours were until 10:00 p.m., so Heather couldn't stay to help Samantha with Zach at night.

"I did end up sending Zach to the nursery on Monday after lots of convincing from Heather...I think he ended up being there for three or four hours. They brought him back when he needed to eat because I had asked the nurses to put a note in his bassinet that said he should not be given a bottle.

"Nursing was kind of hard. I would put him up to the breast, and he would just hang out there. He wasn't latching on for very long...The nurses tried to help. They suggested putting sugar water on my nipples to help 'motivate' Zach to eat. I did try, but it didn't seem to make any difference...He didn't lose weight, but it didn't feel like he was getting a lot, because he would nurse a little and then fall asleep. I hadn't really thought about it [nursing] before. Just thought babies knew how to do this."

At Home

Tuesday afternoon, Samantha and Zach went home. "The early days are sort of a blur. Zach was eating every three hours, so I would wake up, feed him, go back to sleep (for maybe an hour or an hour and a half) and then start over. I started putting Luna energy bars by the bed since it was something good to eat...I was surprised by the shear 'nonstopness' of parenthood. I still caught myself planning about a time to sleep in late or some other luxury. I knew intellectually that this was a nonstop journey, but still at times I thought about it as a short-term thing...Those first few months were hard because he didn't do anything or give back, and I was putting so much into him.

"What taking care of a baby means in daily life is different than what you think while pregnant. When you're not used to someone being dependent on you all the time, it's a shock. Since you're constantly up every three hours and then up at 6:00 a.m. every day, you have to plan more. You can't be spontaneous and have to always keep the baby's schedule in mind. You have to think about whether you will have to feed him while you're out and how that is going to work. Zach also wouldn't always sleep wherever we went, so you have to be home at naptime. I didn't listen to that at first and didn't want to be a slave to his schedule."

Samantha's breastfeeding struggles continued. "Zach would suck on your finger, but when he was at the breast, he wouldn't suck. We had a doula come for a postpartum visit that first week, and she helped with breastfeeding. It helped to talk with her about how we were feeling and what we were doing and have her tell us that Zach was fine, and we were doing the right things...It was important to me that I breastfeed, and I didn't want to give up. If I hadn't been so determined, I would have quit. I can totally see why people end up giving a bottle. Nobody really tells you that it could take a while and be frustrating.

"I did have some nipple pain, but it wasn't excruciating. I would apply lanolin after I nursed...At times, Zach would be crying and I wanted to say to him, 'It's okay. If you just stopped crying, you could latch on.' He could also get wobbly, and it would be hard to get him to hold still...Luckily, every time we went to the doctor, he had always gained weight. I would have been more stressed if he was losing."

Bonding

"I had times of being overwhelmed, especially related to breastfeeding. I felt like I was in 'survival mode' for a while. I was feeding and taking care of him because it was what I needed to do, but I didn't feel the 'I love him more than anything else' feeling. Because of the lack of sleep, I wasn't feeling a whole lot. I really was going through the motions without the strong emotions you are told you'll have.

"I didn't have a strong emotional attachment to breastfeeding. I knew that it was what I wanted to do because it is, I believe, the best way to nourish the baby, but it wasn't an instant emotional bond. If anything, it was a little of the opposite because I felt overwhelmed that it was a part of parenting that was solely my responsibility."

"Other people, like my mom and aunts, had said that breastfeeding is such a great bond. I just felt like, okay, I'm feeding him. A co-worker said to me, 'Oh, don't you just love him more than anything else?' I did love him, but wasn't having the emotional response that I thought I was suppose to have. The media portrays it as if you're instantly in love with them."

Moving Around

When Zach was nine days old, Heather had to go back to Oregon. Her teaching position in California stipulated that she finish her Ph.D. dissertation by the fall, and she needed to work closely with her advisor in Oregon to do that. Samantha, Anna (Samantha's cousin), and Zach joined her there when Zach was three weeks old.

"We had more of a support system in Oregon because we had lived in California less than a year. We rented a place in Oregon for the summer, but Anna, Zach, and I only stayed a month because I had to go back and work at my job (in California) from August tenth through the fifteenth. After working those five days, which completed a year of employment, I was eligible for a six-month family leave." Samantha is a preschool teacher.

During those early months, "I slept whenever Zach did and just didn't plan anything except going to the doctor and things you had to do. When I had the opportunity to sleep, I took it. I was so tired. I didn't want to do anything hard. If I had a burst of energy, I would do something. I would get to the point though where I felt like we had to get out of the house if we hadn't been out for days."

All the moving around was stressful, but Samantha says it was "worth it." "We only saw Heather at night when we were in Oregon, but we had a lot of support. I don't have any regrets about it. Anna would say, 'Here, you need a snack,' and be sure to give me breaks...I had times when I had to give Zach to Anna and take a walk or take a nap.

"My relationship with Heather was a little strained, but mostly because she had to work so much those first few months, and I needed her to be with me." Heather finished her dissertation in time to keep her job and returned to California in late August.

Adjusting To Life With Baby

"It wasn't until Zach was around four to six weeks old that breastfeeding felt totally comfortable...That is when he consistently latched on correctly...Even in breastfeeding class they don't tell you it could take a month or longer.

"I was lucky to have friends and family who were supportive and listened when I needed to talk. There were a few strangers that were critical of how early I was out in public with the baby, or that I didn't have a hat and socks on him in the middle of the summer, but I didn't take any of that to heart. It was interesting how people feel they need to share their advice with you, and you don't even know them.

"Heather and I had to make a conscious effort to make time to be together without taking care of Zach. We could get short with each other, but we didn't have any major blowouts...At times, I would say to Heather, 'I need to go out and you need to stay with Zach. You've had your turn away, now I need to not be a mom for a while.'

"If there is any way you can have another person with you those first few weeks, especially if your partner is back at work, then ask for and accept help. Don't feel you need to do it alone for those eight hours a day. Someone to help take care of you while you take care of the baby is huge...We've already told Anna she needs to have a job that she can take some time off from so she can come help with the next baby!"

Parenting Issues

Since Heather had to work so much in the months after Zach's birth, Samantha felt at times that Heather didn't get how hard it is to be home with a baby. "When Zach was six months old, Heather stayed home with him for a month and that evened things out," she says. "Now we both initiate getting things done. When you're not dealing with it, you don't get it. Some of it is maternal instinct, but some is trial and error.

"We want to be sure that Zach has a strong identity of who he is. Both Heather and I wonder what's going to happen when he goes to school...I wonder what people will think when we put down the names of the parents on a form. You have to find people who are okay with it. I don't want Zach treated differently because of us. As he gets older, I'm sure it will be more of an issue."

As far as her and Heather's relationship, Samantha says, "Having a baby affects your relationship in ways you don't think it would...I knew while pregnant that it meant less time together for the two of us, but not really to what extent. We were also in a situation where we were new to the area so we didn't have a lot of access to babysitters, and I had thought—you just get a babysitter and then you can have some time together...It's funny because everything sounds so duh! now. Of course we have less time together. Of course we have different roles now that we are partners in making decisions for how to raise this child. You just have more details to figure out...I think the biggest thing is that I see myself as a mother first and a partner/wife second. That surprised me. Not that I have to choose which one is first or second, but the reality of life and energy is that the energy has to go to the baby first and then to yourself."

AUTHOR'S REFLECTIONS

When my first daughter was a month old, unexpectedly the owners of the home we were renting put the house on the market. The thought of having to move soon, along with the stress of potential homebuyers tromping through the house at all hours, sent my stress level through the roof. Thankfully, after a few weeks, the owners decided not to sell, and we were free to stay and rent for another year.

When I think about all the moving around that Samantha and her family did those first months of Zach's life, I'm impressed by how they managed it. I don't know if I could have done it with a new baby in tow.

I like what Samantha said about things evening out after Heather stayed home with Zach a month. I've often thought that if both parents had the opportunity to be home with a newborn for a chunk of time, then our rates of divorce would drop. Conflict so often arises with new parents when one person doesn't understand the difficulties of being home with a baby. Whenever someone told me, "Isn't it nice you get to stay home?" I wanted to say, "Why don't you come over and try it for a day after being woken up four to five times the night before?" It seemed that so many people (men and women) didn't get how relentless caring for a baby can be. Once you do "get it," you understand the great benefit of having someone there to help, like Samantha had with Anna. Every new parent deserves an Anna.

CHAPTER ELEVEN

Lisa: "You Have To Accept That Life Is Different"

A common misconception in American culture is that if you are in a stable relationship, your finances are good, and your pregnancy is planned, then you shouldn't have any problems adjusting to a new baby. Lisa is one of millions of women who thought she was prepared for the arrival of her first child. She and her husband, Chris, had been happily married for almost two years. They both had successful careers and were excited about bringing a baby into their lives. "I had no fears or trepidations about being a mother." Lisa says. "I thought I knew what was in store."

Lisa miscarried after her first conception and then "bled for eight weeks." Her second conception luckily took. At twenty-six weeks, Lisa had contractions from premature labor and spent sixteen hours in the hospital. "They gave me an anti-contraction medicine that was adrenaline producing. My heart rate went up, and I was sweating and vomiting."

The attending doctor sent Lisa home with orders to stay on bed-rest until she saw her obstetrician (OB). Four days later, Lisa's OB took her off bed-rest. He said that there was no research that actually showed that bed-rest would stop premature labor. The rest of the pregnancy went fine. "I did still have some contractions at home—possibly Braxton-Hicks ones—and some shooting pains in my legs at times. But I never had to go back into the hospital until the birth."

Lisa read books instead of taking classes to prepare for the delivery. "I read, *What to Expect When You're Expecting*, *The Girlfriend's Guide to Pregnancy*, and *The Illustrated Book of Pregnancy and Baby Care*. I would see birth pictures, but didn't connect it to me. I also didn't think about my own postpartum. I didn't pack the fridge or do other things."

Lisa's in-laws wanted to come up immediately after the birth. "My friends advised me not to do it. I asked Chris to tell his mom to stay at a hotel, but he wouldn't. So I caved and said they could stay at our house for two days."

In The Hospital

Lisa had a nineteen-hour labor, which included bad back labor. Back labor is when the baby's back is against the mother's spine instead of in the preferred position of the baby's back facing the front or side of the mother's abdomen. With back labor, there is often no relief from pain between contractions.

"Making me lie on my back was the worst part. I let it go on for a while and didn't say anything. The nurses didn't pay too much attention to me." When Lisa was dilated to three centimeters, she received an epidural. She was given a second dose of the medication when the labor dragged on. Baby Abby arrived on a Thursday, two days after her due date, weighing seven pounds, ten ounces.

"I remember my mother-in-law, Liz, making a beeline to the baby and unswaddling her when she was twenty minutes old. Liz didn't congratulate me or ask permission to do that. I also remember immediately feeling better [physically] at birth. I had no more pain. It was weird to go from such discomfort and effort to just feeling like you did nine months earlier. It was a very dramatic transition from being big and pregnant to not being that way."

After the family was cleaned up, they were moved to a private room. "I was irritated by all the interventions—people banging on the door, the constant interruptions. Someone even accidentally came in at midnight. The next baby, I will put a sign on the door, 'Mother Sleeping. Don't come in unless you have specific instructions from the doctor.' I would also keep the baby in the nursery. I woke up at Abby's every noise."

Lisa found herself getting anxious and sleep-deprived in the hospital. Her stress level was building. "I felt surreal and disconnected from reality. There was so much going on around me. I started to freak out about bringing the baby home and felt like my life was over. I was overwhelmed at the thought of not leaving the house or doing anything alone again. Before, we had done whatever we wanted. We traveled to Europe, got married, honeymooned, and moved all in two years. Now I felt trapped. I didn't talk to Chris in the hospital about it, and I just felt so ashamed."

On Saturday, Lisa and her family waited all day for a pediatrician check so they could be released from the hospital. "We hadn't checked in advance if our pediatrician had hospital privileges, and she didn't. We had to wait for the on-call pediatrician."

Frustration At Home

The family arrived home around 9:00 p.m. Saturday night. Lisa's in-laws were waiting at the house, as was Lisa's sister, Sarah. Liz had asked Sarah not to bring her kids over, so Sarah went back to her own home later in the evening.

"I can't remember how much Abby cried that first night, but I think she might have slept in about four-hour chunks," Lisa says. "I do remember that she woke very early on Sunday and cried for a long time, and we were very frustrated. I know now that she was probably hungry, or needed soothing, but I didn't put her on the breast. The breastfeeding was just so new and weird at that point, that it didn't feel natural to stick her on so frequently.

"That first day when you leave the hospital, you have an unbelievable amount to learn: how to change diapers, work the Diaper Genie, care for the umbilical cord, breastfeed, work the car seat, swaddle the baby, recognize the baby's different cries. It's such a steep learning curve. On top of that, you also may be feeling like you're a bad mother."

Family Strains

At 7:00 a.m. Sunday morning, Liz knocked on Chris and Lisa's bedroom door. When they opened the door, Liz just stared at them and didn't say anything. Lisa finally said, "We're okay. We'll see you downstairs."

"I felt so stressed about Abby," she adds. "I was thinking—what's wrong? Why is this baby crying so much? I was also stressed about her not peeing. Those early days, I struggled like everything was life or death. I felt I had no skills and no perspective about caring for a newborn.

"I ended up sending Chris and Liz for formula that Sunday because my milk hadn't come in, and I was worried that Abby would get dehydrated. I wish someone had said, 'Just get some formula. Quit stressing about it.' When they got back, Liz handed the six-pack of formula to me. She shoved the cans in my face. She was always against breastfeeding and very insensitive to what was going on.

"I felt I had to tend to Liz's emotional needs. We were building a new house at the time, and Chris and I went to see it that Sunday. I felt good physically and just needed to get away from Liz for a while."

Unfortunately, Chris had had the flu two weeks before Abby's birth and couldn't take more time off from work. He has a three-hour round trip commute to his job and had to return to work on Monday morning. The tension with Lisa's in-laws was becoming too much. "I told Chris, 'I want them gone.' I told them that I didn't need them anymore and used the excuse that my mom was going to come and help. They left on Tuesday. I was relieved when they were gone. My mom came briefly on Tuesday...She provided mostly moral support and lots of advice."

Crying Escalates

When Abby was two weeks old, she started crying "all day. I was nursing every two hours. I wasn't asking Chris to help during the night because he was working full-time. I would hand off the baby to Chris when he got home though. One day, I called Chris at work crying. He said, 'We need to get help,' and suggested calling his mother back to help."

This time, Lisa told Chris that he had to set parameters with Liz. He told his mom that they needed her to walk the baby, take the baby out, and cook..."It worked out," Lisa says. "She knew what she needed to do and helped for about four days. Chris and I actually went out one evening alone then."

100

Abby's excessive crying continued. "We tried putting her on the dryer, the swing, driving her around, the pacifier, swaddling, walking her, rocking her. She was a classic colicky baby. I was thinking, 'Oh my God, my life is over, and I'm stuck with this horrible, screaming baby.' I didn't like Abby. I had terrible anxiety. If she wasn't asleep, I was anxious. I also felt like I couldn't survive it at times. I remember Chris stayed home one day from work, and he was so frustrated with the crying that he said, 'Jesus Christ, it takes two adults to take care of one baby!' There were days when I felt like it took three."

Lisa's father, a physician, noticed that Lisa was depressed. "We knew it was more than the baby blues," Lisa says, "because I couldn't stop crying. I also couldn't eat and was down to my pre-pregnancy weight within two weeks after birth. I would rather sleep then eat. I felt like I was grieving the loss of my old life."

Postpartum Depression

Lisa called her OB's office and talked to the nurse about her depression. "The nurse said, 'Well, the doctor doesn't deal with these issues.' I couldn't believe how hard it was to get help.

"I was eventually able to get in to see a psychiatrist at four-weeks postpartum and get medication. I started taking Zoloft, and it worked pretty quickly—within seven days. I didn't go to therapy because I didn't feel the need, and I would have had to pay for it out of pocket...I did experience two side effects from the Zoloft—no libido and weight gain. I gained ten pounds. I took Zoloft until Abby was four months old and then switched to Wellbutrin, which helped with the libido issues. I stopped the Wellbutrin when Abby was six months old and haven't had a bout of depression since.

"I feel like those early days with Abby were ruined—that I was cheated. If I get depressed again, I will take medication right away if needed. I wanted to come home with my newborn and enjoy it. I wish I had scheduled all day help for three days a week and that Chris had had more leave."

Unfortunately, Lisa's doctors hadn't reviewed her family's depression history when she was pregnant. If they had, maybe she would have been told that she was at risk for postpartum depression. "My brother is manic-depressive and suffers a lot, but is highly functioning. Other family members had suffered from depression, and I had had a period of depression in my late twenties.

"I would call my sister, Sarah, when I felt bad. She would come over and look at the baby and help me figure out what was wrong. It gave me some perspective. Sometimes, you just had to let Abby cry. It was hard to recognize different cries, and I had so many feelings of being a bad mother because it was so hard."

Some Relief

Sarah would watch Abby so Chris and Lisa could relax. "I had to have breaks. I felt I didn't have a choice, plus I totally trusted Sarah to watch the baby. Someone would have to take Abby out of the house so I could sleep. I couldn't unwind if I felt I had to respond to her cries. Plus, I was so disappointed in my OB and society in general about addressing postpartum depression."

When Abby was four weeks old, Lisa contacted a postpartum doula whose name she obtained from the local baby store. She arranged for the doula to come twice a week for three hours at a time. "It was also helpful to hear other mother's stories at mother's groups. I would feel good about Abby after going to those groups."

The media images of new mothers disturbed Lisa during those early months. "They show new mothers glowing. The reality is a drag—baby on breast, constantly changing diapers, keeping the house up, not seeing adults, worrying about your job, and lack of income. You are on call twenty-four hours a day, which is a constant source of stress. We all survive, but to really enjoy it, that's a luxury."

What also bothered Lisa was that no one had told her how long it would take to establish a routine with a baby. "I would always forget something when I went out of the house with Abby. It took months to get a system down, and a solid year before I was comfortable with a routine."

Lisa's Marriage

Chris was very loving and supportive of Lisa during postpartum, but the stress of parenting a newborn strained their marriage at times. "We could get snappy at each other, cranky, and more critical of each other. Chris would see me have strong reactions to things because of the stress and not know how to react himself. I remember there was a heavy bin of computer stuff that I wanted Chris to move and, when he didn't, I yelled at him. His response was to lift it up in anger, like The Hulk would. We were able to laugh about that eventually.

"What helped was talking about what was going on...If we were trying to get too much done we would say, 'Let's stop working and do something fun as a family.' You have to learn to go with the flow of things. It's a learning process as parents and as a couple."

Tips For Moms

"You have to find resources of people you trust, like a mother nurse or doula, and be okay asking for help. Get that information while you're pregnant so it's at your fingertips. You can't predict the emotional changes you'll go through. Don't be surprised about feeling unhappy when you deal with this huge change; it's bigger than anything. You have to accept that life is different.

"When the baby is little and sleeps most of the time, take advantage of people helping so you can reconnect with your spouse. You'll probably be too tired to care about intimacy, but you need to rest and reconnect with each other. The husband needs attention, too. You will feel like you are leading separate lives in the beginning, but that passes.

"I wish all new mothers knew that it's okay to get help and to give themselves a break by spending time away from the baby. They also need to be able to recognize the signs of postpartum depression. It's okay not to do it all by yourself. It should take a village. You don't have to be a Super Mom. It's easy to fall into that trap, especially with breastfeeding. It does get easier when the baby settles down and naps regularly, but don't be surprised if you're blown away by how difficult it is in the beginning."

AUTHOR'S REFLECTIONS

Lisa gave birth to her second daughter, Meredith, when Abby was a year and a half old. This time she planned for her own needs and things went much more smoothly.

"I had a postpartum visit scheduled with the doctor, just in case I had the same depression. I knew almost immediately after Meredith was born though that I was not depressed (that's how fast it had kicked in for me with Abby), so I cancelled it. I already had a nanny to take care of Abby, so I just kept her on board, which was a great help.

"Chris took off a whole month and did stuff around the house (a huge help) and took care of Abby. That left me to take care of Meredith and to try to catch up on my sleep...With Meredith, I never worried that she was on the breast too much. Whenever she was fussy, I'd nurse her. It felt so much more natural the second time.

"I did get to enjoy the time with Meredith that I felt I didn't get with Abby. The sleep deprivation does still take its toll though. I remember feeling pretty tired and stressed at about eight weeks when I had been the only person who had fed Meredith in that time period. It got better after that, when she tapered off on her feedings."

Although caring for a newborn is never easy, lining up help made a big difference with Lisa's second baby. If every pregnant woman arranged for postpartum support, I believe we would see a lot more happy new moms—and dads, too! I hope Lisa's story will encourage expectant parents to map out a plan that meets the needs of all family members during this time of great emotional adjustment.

CHAPTER TWELVE

Karen: "I Was So Angry At My Body For Quitting On Me."

After trying to conceive for over two years, which included fertility treatments, Karen found herself pregnant with twins. "I remember being excited and terrified all at the same time when I contemplated being a mother," she says. "Would I be a good mom? Would I be patient? How would I handle illnesses, issues, and other problems that come with babies?"

A Complicated Pregnancy

"I started bleeding heavily at around eight weeks pregnant and thought I was having a miscarriage," Karen says. The unexplained bleeding continued for six more weeks. During the sixth month of pregnancy, Karen started having preterm contractions. At twenty-seven weeks, she was put on bed-rest for the rest of the pregnancy.

"I could get up and shower and make one trip downstairs every day. My brother was born three-months premature, and my mother told me, 'You don't want to have an infant in ICU [the Intensive Care Unit.] You'll feel guilty.' I just accepted that I would have to do what I had to do. I couldn't imagine leaving the babies in the hospital."

Eric, Karen's husband, worked from home during her entire bed-rest, and Karen's mother came over to make dinner every night. "My in-laws pitched in too, so I had to learn to relinquish control while still pregnant. Maybe they wouldn't do things the way I would do it, but otherwise it wouldn't get done. It could be awkward at times though—like when my mother-in-law was washing my bras! It did help that by the time the babies came, I could give up control."

The doctors had Karen in and out of the hospital for monitoring, usually three times a week. One twin was a pound heavier than the other so the doctors were concerned about Vanishing Twin Syndrome where a twin siphons nourishment off the other. After a month of monitoring, Karen refused to go in for tests anymore. "It was such a hassle because I'm in New Jersey and the hospital is in Pennsylvania, along with the stress of the tests. I finally said to hell with it. All that testing makes you crazy."

Karen's legs and abdomen were very swollen from carrying twins. "My skin was shiny and tight. One morning I was sure the swelling had split my ankle open because I was bleeding. Turns out I had just cut myself shaving!"

Last Few Weeks Of Pregnancy

At week thirty-four, Karen began suffering "hard labor pains every three or four minutes around the clock." Since Karen wasn't dilated, her doctor wouldn't prescribe pain medication. "I don't think she felt it was necessary...The pain was excruciating. I wanted to throw my body out the window...I did have a prescription for Tylenol with codeine from a prior instance when one baby was lying on my groin (Oh my God, that was the most horrendous pain!). When I got the hard contractions, I took the Tylenol with codeine, but it didn't help. The only relief I got was by standing in a warm shower and letting the water hit my body. I was taking about four hour-long showers a day.

"I was scheduled for a cesarean section but, because I was only thirty-seven weeks along, my ob/gyn wouldn't perform it unless I had an amniocentesis to determine if the babies' lungs were fully developed. I didn't want that amnio for anything because I'd heard horror stories of where the doctor accidentally punctured the sacs with the babies. I recall thinking that this was a very likely possibility since there were two babies in there, and they were both extremely active.

"I told the doctor to check me to see if I was dilated because the labor pains had been so intense for so long...Sure enough, I was dilated to four centimeters and, since I was in really intense pain, she figured it was okay to forego the amnio and just move into surgery."

Connor and Aaron were born on November 12, 2002, a Tuesday afternoon. The babies weighed a healthy six pounds, four ounces (Connor) and seven pounds, seven ounces (Aaron.)

First Night

"The first night in the hospital, I couldn't get any sleep. The nurse told me the only thing I could have was a shot of morphine for pain. I didn't want the morphine since the previous time I'd had it, it made my blood pressure plummet...So she gave me Percocet [a pain reliever] orally. Well, the Percocet upset my stomach, and I started throwing up. I spent the rest of the night nauseous and dry heaving. It was horrible. I couldn't stop crying because I was in so much pain and was so nauseated, and they wouldn't give me anything for the nausea.

"The good thing was I had this sweet nurse come in the next morning. She was irate that the night nurse hadn't called a doctor to see if another drug could have been given to me for pain...After that, she brought me anti-nausea meds and came in every two hours and re-injected the IV with pain medication. She was wonderful."

Bell's Palsy

Wednesday night in the hospital, Karen got up to brush her teeth and "something didn't seem right when I spit out toothpaste. I was so drugged up, I didn't know what it was." On Thursday, Karen's mom told her, "Something is wrong with your face." Her mom brought in a nurse, and the nurse ran out of the room. "All of a sudden, the room was buzzing with doctors," Karen says. "They were afraid I had had a stroke and brought in a neurology team."

Karen was sent to have a cat-scan and the doctors determined that she had Bell's Palsy. The muscles in her face had frozen due to trauma from either the swelling in pregnancy, the c-section, or both.

Bell's Palsy is not a disease. It occurs when abnormal movement or paralysis of the face results from infection, injury, or tumors. Along with the Bell's Palsy, the doctors also found that Karen was very iron-depleted, which made her even more fatigued. "I was really upset that I couldn't bond much with the twins in the hospital...After all I had gone through with in-vitro fertilization, getting pregnant with twins, having a very difficult pregnancy, having a c-section, and then to get Bell's Palsy two days after the boys were born...I was so angry at my body for quitting on me."

A night nurse in the hospital helped Karen prepare for recovery from the Bell's Palsy. The nurse's boyfriend, a very healthy guy, had had Bell's Palsy, and the nurse told Karen that it had wiped him out. "She told me to get as much sleep as possible and as much help as possible. I was just so exhausted, but I couldn't sleep...I also sent the babies to the nursery in the hospital, something I thought was an awful thing to do when I was pregnant, but my friend encouraged me to take advantage of that. I was really afraid of being overwhelmed once I got home with not sleeping." It took a month for Karen's Bell's Palsy to clear up.

Coming Home

Four days after birth, Karen and the boys went home. "My first few weeks at home were rough...I was on a load of medications: steroids and anti-viral medicine for the Palsy, iron pills for the low iron counts, and Zantac for my stomach so I wouldn't be sick from the other meds. And they all had to be taken at various times throughout the day with and without food."

All the twins' grandparents live within ten minutes of Karen's home. "I felt bombarded with visitors. Now I realize that everyone was just being kind, but, at the time, I was quite sad that, again, I didn't really have time alone with the boys...As if people couldn't give us a few weeks to settle in as a family...I felt that my in-laws came over every day, but weren't very helpful and weren't doing things the way I wanted them done. I suppose I was being fussy, but I wanted my own time to bond with the babies.

"Eric's family can be very overbearing, and I didn't grow up with that. I found it suffocating while dating and at other times. When they came over, no one gave a crap about me. Plus, I knew I looked horrible from the Bell's Palsy. They would just say, 'Where are the babies?' It really bothered me, and I'm sure the hormones made it worse. They constantly wanted to be with us, and there were constant phone calls. Eric and I would fight about it, and I would say, 'I don't want your family coming over every day'...When they came over, it felt like they were guests and I had to play hostess. I'm sure my mother probably did annoy Eric at times too, but I can ignore it or fight with her.

"The first few weeks, I was too weak to deal with managing visitors, so I just let it happen. Eventually I told people that coming over for an hour was fine. Or I coordinated it so people came at the same time. Or we would say, 'We're having a Family Day,' which meant no visitors."

Guilt About Not Breastfeeding and Exhaustion

"I would stay upstairs with the babies, and Eric would go downstairs and make bottles...My mother came most days to do our wash, straighten up, and make us dinner." Karen's mom also grocery-shopped and ran errands when Eric couldn't get out. "She helped with the babies and helped take care of me. I felt that I wouldn't have survived without her."

Because of the steroids she was taking, the doctors advised Karen not to breastfeed since the medicine would cross into her milk. "I remember feeling awful about giving it up [Karen had breastfed for a few days in the hospital.] I also felt like I was a lesser person because I wasn't breastfeeding the boys, but I had a lot of cheerleaders in my family and my husband who told me that I needed to just concentrate on getting better.

"At a week old, Aaron had lost a pound, so the doctor said we had to get the boys on a three-hour schedule. That was rough. They were put on a formula for premature babies, and we would set the clock for every three hours. So, for example, we would get up at midnight to feed them, and it would take until 1:30 to finish. Then we had to get up again at 3:00. That went on for about a month, and then the boys started sleeping from twelve to four. The grandparents helped with the night feedings some, but I was too tired to pay bills, get food, or anything else."

Emotional Ups And Downs

"I remember feeling undying love for my sons and understanding why mother animals protect their babies in the wild— that raw, animalistic instinct to protect...I also was terribly afraid that something horrible would happen to them.

"I also remember feeling as though, once the babies arrived, not many people cared about me. It was all about the babies. Not that I was jealous, but I was wondering if I was only a vehicle to house children and, once the boys came, I was left out in the cold."

Karen would argue with her mother whenever a baby was sick. "She would tell me all the things she would have done if she was taking care of the baby. And I would get very upset with this. In one fight I remember saying, 'Why don't you just sue me for custody? Everything I do you're critical of.' My mom said, 'I didn't realize it. You're a wonderful mother.' Then I said, 'Well, you could say it once in a while!'

"A few times, I have had to blatantly say, 'You know, Mom, you act like I'm an unfit mother. I'm quite capable of taking care of these babies.' And that has been enough for Mom to realize she is overstepping her bounds. I suppose that I have learned to speak up for myself and defend my decisions even when others don't agree with them. I've realized that when it's all said and done, I'm still the mother here, and no one else can tell me what to do.

"I kind of thought that once I had a baby, I would have all the answers to every problem. But, I didn't. So I began to rely on my gut feelings about things, and I have trusted my conscience ever since."

Isolation And Perfectionism

"I did suffer the baby blues. I would get really upset and start crying over little things. A sappy TV commercial could make me collapse into a fit of crying." Since the babies were born in the winter, and the weather was bad, Karen didn't want to take the boys out much and risk exposing them to germs. "I felt very much shut-in and lonely and sleep deprived. I also wondered if I was a good enough mother for Connor and Aaron.

"I have a friend whose child died at age six who told me, 'Don't neglect your kids.' I think about her when it's raining, and I can't get out and the kids are driving me crazy. My worse day is nothing like her best day.

"I'm not a very patient person and can get caught up in chores. I have to stop myself. I have to remind myself—so the dishwasher doesn't get unloaded, so what?...I have perfectionist tendencies, and I had worked on those already in the marriage. [Karen and Eric had been married three and a half years when the boys were born.] Bed-rest gave me the opportunity also to let go of those tendencies...I have a friend who is expecting who is a perfectionist. I said to her, 'Go on anything that's convenient for you. If you're not thrilled with your mother-in-law, but she offers you dinner, go for it. You can't have everything perfect.'"

Marital Strains

Family issues continued to stress Karen's marriage. "Eric is a conflict avoider. I had to learn to place boundaries. I started saying no to things like my sister-in-law wanting to come over with her kids or the families wanting to go out to dinner. Eric would say, 'The sisters are mad,' and I would say, 'I don't give a shit.'... I'm sure the family thought I was insane.

"I was feeling suffocated by Eric's family, and he didn't see it that way. I started seeing a therapist to discuss my issues about my in-laws, but I didn't care for the therapist and I only went a few sessions. I even threatened my husband with divorce because I couldn't stand the way I was feeling smothered by his family. The first six months were really hard.

"Finally, I came to the conclusion that we would have to pick and choose our events carefully. Like, we would not go to every single event that they invited us to. Or if they wanted to come over three times, we might only allow them to visit twice. Things did get better. A lot of times, when they come to visit, I make it an opportunity to go out and get errands done like grocery shopping. This way, they get to visit, and I don't feel overwhelmed."

More Medical Issues

When the boys were three months old, Karen experienced more medical complications. During the second of two very painful menstrual periods since the boys' births, she went to the emergency room. The doctors thought it was her appendix, and it could rupture, so they took it out. "I had just started feeling better from the births and had begun getting our lives in order and then I had to have more abdominal surgery. I was very depressed," Karen says.

"I called an on-call doctor one night about three nights after the surgery and was in tears because I was in so much pain. He told me that I was doing too much. I said, 'But I haven't been doing anything strenuous.' He told me, 'You have young twins, and I'm willing to bet you are doing way more than you think. Take it easy.' So I took my pain meds more religiously and within a couple of weeks, I was feeling a lot better."

Unfortunately the surgery did not improve Karen's periods. "Nothing has helped dull the pain, which I have about two to three days per month. I take a high dose of Motrin at that time of the month, but that doesn't help. I have tried a lot of different meds, but with no relief. The doctor's only suggestion is birth control pills, which I'm not interested in because of high breast cancer risks in my family and infertility on my husband's side." Karen eventually found out that she has endometriosis, a condition in which the tissue that normally lines the uterus grows in other areas of the body.

Around the time of the appendix surgery, Karen's mom suggested that Karen might have postpartum depression. "I fought it until the boys were nine months old. I would get bad premenstrual syndrome and would be yelling at everyone. I finally called the doctor and started taking the lowest dose of Zoloft. A month later, I noticed a difference. It took the edge off and my PMS was better."

What She Wishes She Had Known

Karen wished someone had told her when she was pregnant that "the postpartum doldrums were very much a normal part of existence after the babies came. I remember thinking that postpartum was really something like Andrea Yates [a Texas mother who suffered from postpartum psychosis and drowned her five children] where you caused harm to others. Instead, postpartum depression seems to be a very natural reaction from the drop of hormones in the body. I wish I'd expected that I wouldn't feel normal again for months physically.

"I also wish I had made more of an effort to line up a friend to go out with one night a week. Just to get out and do something for myself away from family...Once you're in the nitty-gritty of parenting, you can get consumed by it. I really needed an hour by myself. I was so consumed with having the babies during pregnancy that I didn't think about my own needs postpartum.

"I think that every mother should take every single amount of help that someone is willing to give. Whether it's a home-cooked meal, a load of laundry, or someone feeding the baby for a change. I think it's a great idea to allow others to ease the burden by letting the new mom have some time alone. If, at any time, the new mom feels stressed or depressed, she needs to be vocal about it."

AUTHOR'S REFLECTIONS

When I think about all the medical challenges Karen faced, I feel overwhelmed. Since recovering from birth is difficult itself (let alone from twins!), to add in Bell's Palsy, iron depletion, postpartum depression, and an appendectomy seems insurmountable.

Karen had to struggle with perfectionist tendencies and learn to let some of them go. I often see new moms pushing themselves to do everything even though they are exhausted. I know I did it too at times after each of my daughters' births. Why do we feel we have to handle it all and are so averse to accepting help?

Dr. Monica Ramirez Basco, a clinical associate professor of psychology and the author of *Never Good Enough: Freeing Yourself from the Chains of Perfectionism*, challenges perfectionists not to oversimplify things. Rather than two extremes—perfection or failure—look for shades of gray.

In her book, Basco profiles a woman who puts tremendous pressure on herself to keep every item of clothing in the house laundered and pressed. Basco asks her to think about under what circumstances she might be 25%, 50%, and 75% satisfied with the laundry.

"You want to catch yourself when you think that a situation is either perfect or not, and question that belief," Basco says. "Maybe 50% or 75% is good enough, and you can live with that. Think about the time and energy it takes to be 100%. Is it worth it? Where do you really function best?"

There is no such thing as the perfect mother. Trying to do everything when you're sleep-deprived and overwhelmed with newborn care is a recipe for frustration and mommy burn-out. Give yourself a break. Be a mom who focuses on her own and her children's needs instead of spending energy striving for perfection.

CHAPTER THIRTEEN

Jennifer D.: "I Have No Regrets About My Postpartum Experience"

A t the time Jennifer became pregnant, she was working as a registered nurse in a Postpartum and Well Baby unit. Through her nursing school and childbirth educator trainings, she had discovered some hospital practices that did not make sense to her.

"In the hospital" she says, "natural childbirth only works when the family is very determined and educated or as a fluke because things went so fast there wasn't time for anyone to intervene...I had met several women who had had their babies at home, and I read more studies about the safety of home birth. I knew that I wanted to birth my baby without much outside intervention, and I felt that home would be the best place for me to do that because my midwife would share the same philosophy."

Jennifer's midwife strongly encouraged her to hire the help of a postpartum doula. She also gave advice about taking time to rest and cuddle with her new baby, not buying lots of unnecessary baby stuff, and not rushing back into regular life.

Jennifer's pregnancy went well, although she was tired and had lots of nausea and vomiting into her second trimester. At her job, the other nurses made sure she took plenty of breaks.

Planning Well

"I knew I wanted to take off the maximum amount of time from work after delivery. I wasn't even sure if I wanted to go back to work at all. I planned to wait and see what it was like being a mom before making any decisions about work."

Jennifer's husband, Alex, planned to take two weeks off after the birth. He and Jennifer arranged for a postpartum doula to come for four hours a day, three times a week during the first two weeks. "Alex's job would be to help take care of us until he went back to work," says Jennifer. "Then we would see how things go and take our time re-entering the world.

"We also organized our room to fit some baby stuff. We were living in a tiny one-bedroom place at the time. We planned on having two weeks as our 'babymoon' when we were going to do hardly any cooking, cleaning, or entertaining...My job was to rest and nurse the baby."

Birth And Processing What Happened

Jennifer went into labor on her due date and almost twenty-four hours later, Naomi was born at home with a midwife, midwife's assistant, birth doula and, of course, Alex in attendance. "The second stage of labor was more challenging than I'd expected, but overall things went well...I will never forget the moment of her birth and the feeling of holding her for the first time while her cord was still connected to me and pulsating.

"My bottom was very sore, and I did have a small tear in the fourchette [perineum]. Naomi latched on to my breast soon after birth and a few hours later fell asleep. She was born around 1:30 a.m., and the midwife and everyone left around 4:00 a.m. The rest of the morning, Alex, Naomi, and I all slept together with Naomi on Alex's chest...I remember Naomi unfolding and stretching out her arms and legs for the first time. We were really happy and peaceful."

Many women have trouble accepting that their birth did not go as they imagined. Jennifer was no different. However, she recovered quickly from that because her birth doula helped her to process what happened. "I had envisioned being upright for birth, but the midwife had me push lying on my side, which was very painful, and then lying on my back. I didn't like it. I did sit up in the end, but I wasn't happy about all the other ways I pushed. My doula afterwards said, 'There's always something that happens (that you don't anticipate.)' That helped me to accept that that's just life. I was happy with my midwife overall, so I had to focus on that."

Jennifer remembers her first days postpartum as "pretty blissful. We just all stayed in bed most of the time and cuddled a lot.

In the photos from that time, we don't look great because our hair is all over the place, my skin is broken out, and we are in our pajamas. I was content and not so worried about the way we looked since we weren't really having any visitors anyway."

Standing Firm On Her Needs

It was hard for Jennifer to tell people that they didn't want visitors for a while. "People were insulted, but I was adamant. I had to take a stand." Some family members also didn't approve of Jennifer having a home birth or of her hiring a postpartum doula. Jennifer's mother said, "You don't need that [the postpartum doula.] You don't have another kid." It turns out her mother had forgotten how much help she had had when her own children were young. For example, Jennifer's grandmother would come over to bottle feed the babies at night so that Jennifer's mother could sleep.

The postpartum doula helped with cooking and shopping, and Jennifer's mother also came some to help. Naomi nursed "pretty much constantly," about every hour-and-a-half. "My nipples were a little sore, but not bad," Jennifer says. "My milk came in on my second day postpartum, and Naomi never lost weight.

"The house wasn't clean, but since we had a one-bedroom, it was actually easier. Even though it was cluttered, it was less space to worry about cleaning."

Lessons Learned During Pregnancy

"I'm grateful for the postpartum advice I did get in my home birth childbirth prep classes and from my midwife. It really made me take it seriously that it was okay, even expected, that Alex and I take time to just rest and get to know the baby after the birth. And to make arrangements to hire, barter, or beg for help with household stuff for at least the first two weeks."

While pregnant, Jennifer also had learned about the Postpartum Clock. On a piece of paper, you draw the face of a clock and then mark off a half hour every two hours for nursing and also mark off estimated blocks of time for diaper changing, showering, eating, and sleeping. Expectant parents can quickly see that it's going to be hard to get other things done and that they shouldn't press themselves to do more than is needed.

Another thing Jennifer did to prepare was to set up all her nursing supplies by her bed. Her doula also suggested that she layer where the baby slept with four sheets and waterproof pads between each sheet. That way Jennifer and Alex wouldn't have to change sheets in the middle of the night if Naomi's diaper leaked.

On Her Own

At two-weeks postpartum, Alex went back to work, and the doula was gone. Alex picked up a lot of the slack to help Jennifer when he was home. Jennifer also didn't pressure herself to do much. She would only go on one outing a day with the baby. Instead of stressing about getting things done she "really fell in love with Naomi and just marveled at her changes."

What was stressful was that Naomi would often cry when they saw other people. "I would go to yoga, and she would cry, but it was still good to see the teacher and other students. I just had to accept that this was the way it is right now. When I would see other moms whose babies weren't crying so much, I would wonder what was wrong. It wasn't like Naomi was a fussy baby, she just could work herself up. I would try to catch it before it got bad. It was funny. She didn't like the baby store, but the grocery store was fine. One time at the grocery store, a man said to me, 'You seem so comfortable with her,' and that helped."

What also helped in those early weeks was that Jennifer had previously assisted other moms with breastfeeding. "I knew what a good latch was and would pull Naomi on and off all the time if she wasn't latched on right. The best advice I can give other moms is to learn as much as you can about breastfeeding while pregnant. There is a lot of misinformation out there. Most doctors and many nurses are misinformed. La Leche League is free and, even though you may not agree with their politics, they know how to breastfeed. Other moms who are experienced in breastfeeding can help. Get help right away if you're having problems. Sometimes you have to talk to more than one person, and you have to be committed to it."

A Medical Complication

At eight-weeks postpartum, Jennifer developed genital prolapse, a condition that occurs when the structures of the pelvis protrude into or outside of the vaginal canal. "This was very scary and unexpected to me. My midwife referred me to my doctor, and my doctor was not very concerned, helpful, or supportive. I think he was annoyed that I called him just a few days before Christmas for an appointment. To me, it was an emergency. I didn't know what caused it or what I could do about it."

Jennifer did more research on her own and ended up paying out of pocket to see a nurse practitioner that a friend had recommended. "I found this condition to be very embarrassing. I was afraid of having sex—that sex would make it worse. I didn't feel very sexy. I thought I was gross. While I can't say that my body is as it was before Naomi was born, it has gotten better. However, I still feel uncomfortable talking about this topic. Like somehow it was my fault and that I should have been able to prevent it if only I hadn't spent most of my life overweight or if I hadn't done so much lifting during pregnancy at work.

"My sex drive did not come back for a long time. That was hard. I have a really strong relationship with my husband, but it is so much more challenging when you have a child. It's just really hard to get dinner done, chores, get the baby to bed, and then have some time to ourselves."

Going Back To Work

Jennifer took five months of maternity leave. She went back to work one night a week then, but decided after three months that it wasn't working for her. "It was crazy to think I could work nights and then take care of Naomi during the day. It took a long time to realize that being an at-home parent is a full-time job. You always think you have more time than you do."

Reflecting back on her postpartum period, Jennifer says, "What I would do differently is have the doula or other people come to help longer. I also would not have gone back to working one night a week at the hospital...But I have no regrets about Naomi's birth or my postpartum experience. I was tired, but I kept perspective...Postpartum can be a joyful experience if the family has the proper support in place. This means that mom is only resting and nursing the baby for at least two weeks (longer if the birth or pregnancy was complicated.) This is not a luxury."

Author's Reflections

It's not often that I come across a woman like Jennifer who has no remorse about her postpartum experience. By arranging for help in advance and focusing on her family's need for rest and support, she was able to see the positives in those early months with Naomi.

There are many things you can do while pregnant to lessen the demands on you postpartum. Freeze meals, like casseroles, in advance. Other easy meals are salads, soups, sandwiches, or even pancakes for dinner. Also, have your local grocery and restaurant delivery phone numbers handy.

Stock your home with non-perishables. You don't want to be running to the store two days postpartum for toilet paper. Paper plates, cups, and plastic utensils will give you a break from dishwashing for a while.

Lower your housecleaning standards during postpartum like Jennifer did. Rest and time to get to know your baby should be the priorities, not cleaning.

Look for ways to simplify household chores before the baby arrives. Clean out clutter so you have fewer things to dust. Organize your house so items are near where you use them. Use a laundry basket system that allows you to sort dirty clothes right when you take them off. For example, in my house, each person has one basket for darks and one for lights.

Wash baby clothes in advance (they can contain chemicals that irritate a baby's skin), but don't wash everything. You probably will have more infant clothes than your baby will ever wear, so set some of them aside to exchange later for bigger clothes or for a store credit.

Set up diaper changing and baby feeding areas on every floor of your house so you're not running up and down the stairs all day. Some nice items for a feeding area are: burp cloths, a water bottle, a breastfeeding pillow, books, a journal—whatever will comfort the parents when they are feeding the baby.

It's okay to set a time limit on visits or say that you won't be having visitors at all until after a certain number of weeks. Answering the door in your bathrobe also gets the message across quickly that you're too tired for socializing! This is your postpartum experience so do what's best for your family.

Be prepared when someone offers support. Think about all the groups you are involved with—places of worship, coworkers, sports teams—and let people know you'd appreciate whatever help they are comfortable providing. This is not a time to turn away assistance. Maybe they would like to help with laundry, watch the baby while you nap, or grocery shop. If you have a friend who is great at organizing, you can even have her arrange your help.

Final Thoughts

You probably noticed some recurring themes in the mothers' stories: breastfeeding doesn't always come easily, new mothers should accept all the help they can get, caring for a baby is a full-time job, planning for your own needs after birth is important, and postpartum hormones can be highly unpredictable. I hope these stories have given you food for thought and helped to open your eyes to the realities of the first year of motherhood.

I challenge you now to find ways to lessen the difficulties of the months after birth for yourself and other moms. If we all can reach out to new mothers and offer them assistance, then early motherhood could be a time of more joy, and fewer regrets, for so many women. New mothers deserve hands-on help, encouragement, and support. What will you do to ensure your needs are met after your baby's birth? What will you do to help other mothers when it is their time?

APPENDIX A

Resources For New Parents

The resources in this section are organized by topic to provide further help with your life as a new parent.

BREASTFEEDING:

Books:

Bestfeeding: Getting Breastfeeding Right for You by Mary Renfrew, Chloe Fisher, and Suzanne Arms. Celestial Arts, 2000.

Nursing Mother, Working Mother: The Essential Guide for Breastfeeding and Staying Close To Your Baby After You Return to Work by Gayle Pryor. Harvard Common Press, 1996.

The Nursing Mother's Companion by Kathleen Huggins. Harvard Common Press, 2005.

The Tender Gift: Breastfeeding by Dana Raphael. Prentice-Hall, 1973.

The Womanly Art of Breastfeeding by La Leche League International. Plume Publishing, 2004.

Organizations/Websites:

Breastfeed.com
www.breastfeed.com

Breastfeeding.com
www.breastfeeding.com

International Lactation Consultants Association
1500 Sunday Drive, Suite 102
Raleigh, North Carolina, 27607
(919) 861-5577
Fax: (919) 787-4916
www.ilca.org

La Leche League International
1400 N. Meacham Road
Schaumburg, IL 60173-4804
(847) 519-7730 or (800) LA-LECHE
www.lalecheleague.org

Nursing Mothers' Counsel (San Francisco/Bay Area)
www.nursingmothers.org

DOULAS/POSTPARTUM CARE:

Books:

After the Baby's Birth: A Complete Guide for Postpartum Women by Robin Lim. Ten Speed Press, 2001.

The Doula Advantage by Rachel Gurevich. Prima Publishing, 2003.

Mothering the New Mother: Women's Feelings & Needs After Childbirth by Sally Placksin. Newmarket Press, 2000.

Mother Nurture: A Mother's Guide to Health in Body, Mind, and Intimate Relationships by Rick Hanson, Ph.D., Jan Hanson, L.Ac., and Ricki Pollycove, M.D. Penguin Books, 2002.

Postpartum Survival Guide by Ann Dunneworld, Ph.D., and Diane G. Sanford, Ph.D. New Harbinger Publications, 1994.

Organizations/Websites:

Childbirth and Postpartum Professionals of America (CAPPA)
(888) MY-CAPPA
www.cappa.net

Doula Network
www.doulanetwork.com/directory

Doula World
www.doulaworld.com

Doulas of North America (DONA)
(888) 788-DONA
www.dona.org

National Association of Postpartum Care Services
(800) 45-DOULA
www.napcs.org

LIFE COACHING:

Claudia Heilbrunn
Life Coach for first-time moms
(212) 222-4394
www.significantself.com
Ms. Heilbrunn offers new clients a free forty-five minute coaching session by phone.

MATERNAL CARE/CESAREAN AWARENESS:

Childbirth Connection
281 Park Avenue South, 5th Floor
New York, NY 10010
(212) 777.5000
Fax: (212) 777-9320

www.childbirthconnection.org
At the website you can download the book, *A Guide to Effective Care in Pregnancy and Childbirth*, for free. You can also download the book, *What Every Pregnant Woman Needs to Know About Cesarean Section*, for a fee.

International Cesarean Awareness Network, Inc. (ICAN)
1304 Kingsdale Avenue
Redondo Beach, CA 90278
(310) 542-6400 or (800) 686-ICAN
Fax: (310) 697-3056
www.ican-online.org

ONLINE PARENTING SUPPORT:

BabyCenter
www.babycenter.com

Moms Club International
www.momsclub.org

National Organization of Mothers of Twins Clubs
www.nomotc.org

One Young Parent (for teen parents)
www.oneyoungparent.com

Postpartum Dads
www.postpartumdads.org

Single Mothers
www.singlemothers.org

PARENTING/LIFE BALANCE BOOKS:

The Girlfriend's Guide to Surviving the First Year of Motherhood by Vicki Iovine. Perigee Books, 1997.

The Happiest Baby on the Block: The New Way to Calm Crying and Help Your Baby Sleep Longer by Harvey Karp, M.D. Bantam Books, 2003 (DVD also available.)

*A Housekeeper is Cheaper Than a Divorce: Why You Can Afford to Hire Help and How to Get I*t by Kathy Fitzgerald Sherman. Life Tools Press, 2000.

If Only I Were a Better Mother: Using the Anger, Fear, Despair and Guilt That Every Mother Feels at Some Time, as a Pathway to Emotional Balance and Spiritual Growth by Melissa Gayle West. Stillpoint Publishing, 1992.

Mothers Who Think: Tales of Real-Life Parenthood. Edited by Camille Peri and Kate Moses. Washington Square Press, 1999.

Operating Instructions: A Journal of My Son's First Year by Anne Lamott. Anchor Publishing, 2005.

Secrets of the Baby Whisperer: How To Calm, Connect, and Communicate With Your Baby by Tracy Hogg. Ballantine Books, 2001.

POSTPARTUM DEPRESSION:

Books:

Beyond the Blues: A Guide to Understanding and Treating Prenatal and Postpartum Depression by Shoshana S. Bennett, Ph.D., and Pec Indman. Moodswings Press, 2003.

Conquering Postpartum Depression: A Proven Plan for Recovery by Ronald Rosenberg, M.D., Deborah Greening, Ph.D., and James Windell. Da Capo Press, 2004.

Down Came the Rain: My Journey Through Postpartum Depression by Brooke Shields. Hyperion, 2005.

The Postpartum Husband: Practical Solutions for Living With Postpartum Depression by Karen R. Kleiman, M.S.W. Xlibris Corporation, 2001.

This Isn't What I Expected: Recognizing and Recovering From Depression and Anxiety After Childbirth by Karen R. Kleiman, M.S.W., and Valerie D. Raskin, M.D. Bantam Books, 1994.

Organizations/Websites:

Postpartum Depression Help
www.postpartumdepressionhelp.com

Postpartum Support International (PSI)
(800) 944-4PPD
www.postpartum.net

APPENDIX B

Postpartum Articles By The Author

Independence: An Essay On Postpartum Depression

Independence has been a blessing and a curse for me. I am a very strong-willed person and don't like to feel dependent on anyone or anything else. This can be a good thing. I pay my bills on time, am respected for being a responsible person, and trust that I can figure out a way to solve my problems. I also am not afraid to travel or do much else alone—in fact, I relish it. I know my streak of independence has been part of why I've tried many things in my life and look forward to more adventures.

The flip side of this desire for independence is the pain it has caused me and my family. Four months after the birth of my second daughter, Linda, I suffered a severe postpartum depression. I couldn't understand why I felt so horrible and, for the first time in my life, considered suicide. The physical pain in my body—the fatigue, raw nerves, and achiness—was more than I could take. I remember one particularly bad day when I collapsed to my knees, crying uncontrollably in the garage so the kids wouldn't see me.

For two months, I hid my pain from my husband. I thought I was losing my mind and must be a horrible mother. You see, it wasn't until Linda was born that I became a stay-at-home mom. Since I felt so awful, I thought I couldn't handle being home with my kids. I yelled at the kids often and just wanted them to leave me alone.

When I finally told my husband, he immediately said we needed to see a doctor. But, I wouldn't go. I was determined to get better on my own. To me, going to seek help showed weakness. A lot of my thinking was due to the depression playing tricks on my thought processes and society's ignorance about depression. Additionally, I had already tried to talk with my primary care doctor, and he had dismissed me. I will never forget his words, "You're probably just upset that the climax of giving birth is over."

In retrospect, what he said was ridiculous. My daughter was five months old at the time of our discussion, and I had long labors that I was thrilled to finish. Having a medical professional ignore my symptoms, unfortunately, convinced me even more that I was going crazy.

Finally, after several more months of pain, I agreed to see a psychiatrist. The doctor wanted to put me on anti-depressant medication right away and into counseling. Again, my stubborn streak appeared, and I refused medication. The thought of having to take medicine scared the hell out of me. I was sure that the next step was a mental institution. I did agree to the counseling, however. It helped a little.

About two months later, my symptoms drastically improved, and I felt somewhat normal for the first time in six months. I have since researched postpartum depression and concluded that when I weaned Linda from breastfeeding too quickly, it threw my body off kilter. It then took almost six months for my body to get back in balance.

Once I was better, I became very angry at myself. I was haunted by the way I had treated my family during the depression. Those months were truly hell in our house. I vowed never to deny myself help when I needed it in the future.

It's a good thing I made that promise because the depression returned approximately two years later. This time, I didn't wait. I sought treatment right away and found that anti-depressants really are necessary for me. Counseling is helpful, but my new doctor agrees that my form of depression is probably ninety percent biological.

It still frightens me that I'm dependent on medication. I keep reminding myself that this is a disease. You wouldn't deny a diabetic insulin, or a cancer patient chemotherapy. When I keep my depression under control with medicine, I am freeing myself and my family from a lot of pain. It's a trade-off I have learned to accept.

New Mom Support List

Don't neglect to prepare for your needs along with your baby's during the postpartum months. Fill in your local contacts on the list below and you'll always be a call away from informational or emotional support. Remember—it takes a village.

New Mom Support List:
Baby Store:
Classmates from your childbirth class:
Dog Walker:
Friends/family who have offered to help:
Grocery Store that delivers:
Housecleaning Service:
Lactation Consultant:
La Leche League: (800) LALECHE or www.lalecheleague.org
Mom with an older child whose parenting you respect:
Neighbors who have offered to help:
New Parent Support Group:
Pediatrician:
Postpartum Doula:
Postpartum Massage Therapist:
Postpartum Support International: (800) 944-4PPD or www.postpartum.net
Restaurants that deliver:

Postpartum Doulas: Nurturing Help For Your Family

It's 8:00 a.m., and you're already wondering how you'll make it through the day. You've been up since 5:30 nursing and rocking your fussy baby after a night of broken sleep. You're not sure how you'll ever take a shower, let alone fix some breakfast. Your body aches from labor and delivery, and you would love a sympathetic shoulder to cry on as well as someone to answer your nagging questions about caring for yourself and your baby.

To the rescue—the postpartum doula. She whisks in, brings you a cup of tea and something to eat, and then takes the baby from your tired arms. You get the chance to rest while someone else handles things for a while. By the time your doula leaves, you've showered, napped, and feel much more confident in your role as a mom.

Why We Need Postpartum Help

Most new parents are caught off guard by how overwhelming the postpartum time can be. During pregnancy, they had read about preparing for a child, attended childbirth and baby care classes, and readied the nursery. Unfortunately, many books and classes for expectant parents don't touch upon the incredible emotional and physical demands of caring for a newborn and why new parents should consider seeking postpartum help.

In their book, *The Postpartum Survival Guide*, authors Ann Dunnewold, Ph.D., and Diane G. Sanford, Ph.D., describe the truth about postpartum. They state, "The reality is that becoming a parent is a considerable task. The new mother's body appears to have gone haywire; her hormones fluctuate greatly. She is tired beyond belief and suffering from sleep deprivation...The new mother is in a physically vulnerable state from these changes and from the enormous physical stress of childbirth. And then, after a couple days' rest, if she's lucky, she is put in charge of meeting another human being's needs before tending to any of her own."

We used to care for postpartum families much differently than we do today. Communities would rally around new families by providing practical help—like bringing meals—and emotional support in the form of mother mentoring from either female relatives or other seasoned mothers in the community. Nowadays, new mothers are often isolated from such support and don't know where to turn for assistance.

Marlo D. Robinson, the President of Mother's Care Doula Services, Inc., says that "first and foremost, parents are just plain scared of having to care for this new, little person... I often joke that there is no call button to press for a nurse to come running once the parent gets home."

What Is A Postpartum Doula?

A postpartum doula provides in-home care, usually for three to four hours at a time, to help new families adjust to life with their baby. You may have heard of birth doulas, but there are also doulas who specialize in postpartum support.

Postpartum doulas care for the baby and older siblings, perform household chores, run errands, provide breastfeeding support, or just let the new mom take a nap or have a good cry. A doula is there to provide emotional, physical, and informational assistance so the mother can focus on resting and bonding with her baby. Doulas can answer your questions about handling a newborn and provide information on local resources for parents. They are also trained to watch for signs of postpartum depression.

As Sally Placksin notes in her book, *Mothering the New Mother*, a doula is "one who nurtures the new mother by performing those tasks that comfort her and free her to be with her baby."

Some doulas offer special expertise such as massage therapy, vegetarian cooking, or babyproofing. There are also doula services that provide overnight care. Fees typically range from $15 to $35 an hour, depending on the doula's level of experience and services provided.

One of the most important things a doula does is listen to a new mother's concerns. Sabrina Flynn, a first-time mom whose mother encouraged her to hire a postpartum doula, says, "The doulas I had were good listeners. They didn't tell me what I should be doing. They just listened to me. It was wonderful."

Postpartum Doula Benefits

In her over ten years of working as a postpartum doula, and helping more than five hundred families, Vicky York has found many reasons for new families to hire a postpartum doula. The benefits include: increased chance of successful breastfeeding, reduced chance of infant dehydration and hospitalization, less chance of maternal exhaustion, reduction in unnecessary calls to the pediatrician, and less anxiety when the partner returns to work since they know mom is receiving help at home.

Cindy Levine-Rind hired Betsy Schwartz of Tenth Month Doula Services as her doula when she came home after the birth of her son, Josh. "I had no idea how difficult it would be," she says of the postpartum time. "Betsy taught me what to do to care for the baby, gave me time to sleep, and to recover from a difficult birth."

When Mimi Selevan underwent a c-section, and then had difficulties with breastfeeding, she decided to contact Mother's Care for help. "With my doula's help, I was able to sleep worry free a few hours in between feedings. I really think this helped me recover quicker. The doula helped with dishes and laundry, and this allowed me to bond more with Sally."

Many parents hire a doula for subsequent babies to help them adjust to the changes every new child brings. Jennifer Davis already had a three-year-old when she gave birth to twins. "There were a lot of nursing issues that came up with the twins that hadn't with my first child," Davis says. "Janet (her doula) was able to help me sort through various options and also hooked me up with a lactation consultant who was very helpful."

Planning For Postpartum Support

If financing a postpartum doula is a budget concern for you, there are ways to work it out. For shower or baby gifts, ask friends and family to donate to a doula fund, or have them purchase gift certificates for doula services. Often doulas can arrange a financing plan for you so that you can spread out your payments. Check with your health insurance provider and with you and your partner's employers to see if compensation for postpartum care costs is available.

Ilyene Barsky, Founder and Director of the The Center for Postpartum Adjustment, advises expectant moms to be optimistic, but realistic. She cautions against allowing everyone to come visit right after the birth. Barsky says, "New moms should plan so that the visitors are spread out over the first few weeks. Maybe at first the husband is home. Then, when he goes back to work, the mother, mother-in-law, or postpartum doula comes. Strive for 4 to 6 weeks of always having another pair of hands there to help."

An Investment In Your Family

Don't hesitate to seek out help during the postpartum period. It's not a sign of weakness, but of strength, to get the nurturing you need during this overwhelming time. You can't give from an empty place, and it won't help anyone if you are depleted. Jane Honikman, the Founding Director of Postpartum Support International, encourages new parents to see hiring a postpartum doula as an "investment" in their families. The payoff is a more confident and rested mom who is better able to tackle motherhood's challenges.

Working Out With Your Baby

You've got your workout clothes on, and you're ready to conquer your first exercise class since giving birth. Then the phone rings. The babysitter needs to cancel. It's enough to make a new mom toss her cross-training shoes right in the trash. But, there is another way. Why not exercise with your baby instead? It's a great way to bond with your child, and you'll be laying the groundwork for a lifetime of healthy fitness habits.

Here are some ideas for getting fit with baby in tow (be sure to get your healthcare provider's approval before starting any exercise program.):

1) Work out to an exercise video while carrying your baby in a sling or snuggly. Lisa Stone, a Pre- and Post-Natal Fitness Instructor and the creator of the Fitfor2 fitness programs (www.fitfor2.com), recommends you choose any pre-pregnancy video that is low impact. For safety, she suggests, "Always keep one hand on the baby—either on the back of the neck, cradling the baby's head, or on the baby's back if they have good neck control." You could also exercise to a video with the baby safely in a seat or playpen nearby.

2) Strength training for your arms. There are lots of ways to strength train with your child—just use your baby instead of hand weights for resistance. Stone suggests two ways to work your biceps:

Biceps Exercise #1: Sitting in a chair, place your baby tummy down, across your right forearm, and hold under their shoulders with your right hand. Use your left hand to hold their left thigh, near the hip socket. Starting with your forearm parallel to the floor, lift the baby up toward your shoulder and repeat reps. Switch arms.

Biceps Exercise #2: Lie on your back, knees bent, hold the baby under his armpits, tummy down, on your chest. Lift the baby straight up in the air above your face as you exhale. Then bring your elbows down towards your sides and plant a kiss on your baby's forehead as you inhale. Don't be surprised if this one brings on lots of giggles!

Triceps Exercise: To work the triceps, Ben Kwock, a certified personal trainer and program coordinator for the YMCA, provides the following exercise: Start in a similar position as Biceps Exercise #2, except begin with your elbows pointing towards the ceiling, holding the baby over your face. Straighten your arms to lift the baby into the air. While keeping your upper arms still, lower the baby's tummy toward the top of your head and back up again.

3) Swimming or water walking with baby. Kwock suggests holding the baby under the arms and then straightening and bending your arms, moving the baby back and forth through the water to work your back and chest. Many pools offer water walking, and you can carry the baby in a snuggly while you walk the shallow lanes. Be sure to get your pediatrician's go-ahead before taking your baby into a chlorinated pool. Also, since a baby needs to be six months old before you can use sunscreen, swim at indoor pools, or make sure the baby is fully covered until the baby reaches that milestone.

4) Stomach crunches. Stone recommends the following exercise: Lie on your back with your knees bent, then place your baby either tummy down on your abdomen, or sit the baby up with his back against your thighs while you hold him with one hand. As you exhale, tighten your abdominal muscles and lift your head and shoulders off the ground while pressing your lower back into the floor. Slowly lower your head to the ground as you inhale. Repeat eight to ten times. Work up to three sets.

5) Hiking with baby in a pack. Hiking is a great cardiovascular workout and an activity that you can continue to share with your children as they grow. It's also a psychological boost to get out and enjoy nature after staring at the same four walls of your house for weeks. The first hikes with your baby should be short, easy trips, and be sure to bring plenty of water and snacks to keep your energy up.

Remember, the baby won't be exercising and will probably need to wear more layers than you to keep warm.

6) Squats, lunges, and calf raises. "A good way to work the quadriceps and gluteal muscles is to hold your baby while doing squats," says Kwock. "Be careful to only go as far as you can comfortably without your knees sticking out past your toes. Back lunges are also good for these areas. To work the calf muscles, hold your baby while you do heel raises." Start with a set of 8 to 12 repetitions per exercise and add sets as you build strength.

7) Postnatal Yoga. Mom and Baby Yoga instructor Penni Thorpe says, "Yoga is a great way to get back in shape after a new baby." If there's not a class in your town, consider purchasing the book, *I Can't Believe It's Yoga for Pregnancy and After*, (Hatherleigh Press, 2000) by certified personal and yoga trainer to the stars, Lisa Trivell.

8) Find an exercise buddy. Okay, I cheated a little bit, since this isn't an exercise. It is, however, one of the best ways to stay motivated. Your buddy can be your spouse, another new mom, your older children, a neighbor, a friend—even your dog! Just knowing that someone else is counting on you to show up can get you out the door.

9) Dancing while holding the baby. Crank up some fun music and dance away. Again, if you are carrying the baby in a snuggly or sling, be sure to keep one hand on the baby at all times, and no jumping.

10) Strollercize or other Mom/Baby exercise classes. Many postpartum exercise classes let you bring your baby along or are designed to use the stroller with baby in it as a resistance tool. Check your local hospital or Park and Recreation department for classes. For information on Strollercize classes or their video workout, go to www.strollercize.com or call (800) Y-STROLL.

11) The most popular form of exercise in America: Walking. Pushing a baby in a stroller or carrying the baby in a pack adds resistance and

helps you burn more calories. A suggestion from other moms: time your walk for right before naptime. After the walk, put the baby down for her nap, do some stretching, and take a nap yourself. You deserve it!

About The Author

Melanie Bowden is a Certified Postpartum Doula. She has provided in-home care to dozens of new families, including families of twins and triplets. Melanie teaches infant massage classes and speaks to parenting groups about postpartum issues. She is also the creator of the workshop *How To Reduce New Parent Stress*. Her magazine articles have appeared in over eighty publications, including *Shape, Jugglezine,* and *Twins*. She teaches writing classes, and is also a mathematics instructor at American River College, a masters swimmer, and a firm believer that you shouldn't talk on your cell phone while driving.

Melanie lives with her husband, two daughters, one neurotic dog, and two semi-destructive cats in Davis, California. This is her first book.

Printed in the United States
61096LVS00002B/364-393